Praise for MAN UP!

"[An] incredible story."

—CBSNewYork.com

"A sweet tale."

—*New York Daily News*

"Not your typical celebrity memoir...While other memoirs strive to be either poignant or funny, this book succeeds with being both...If you're looking for a great, light-hearted, and funny read, look no further than MAN UP! Find out why America loves him so much...You will not be disappointed."

—*Viva Glam Magazine*

MAN UP!

Tales of My Delusional Self-Confidence

Ross Mathews

A Chelsea Handler Book / Borderline Amazing® Publishing

GRAND CENTRAL
PUBLISHING

NEW YORK   BOSTON

Grand Central Publishing
Hachette Book Group
237 Park Avenue
New York, NY 10017

www.HachetteBookGroup.com

A Chelsea Handler Book/Borderline Amazing® Publishing

Printed in the United States of America

RRD-C

First trade edition: February 2014
10 9 8 7 6 5 4 3 2

A Chelsea Handler Book/Borderline Amazing® Publishing is an imprint of Grand Central Publishing.
Grand Central Publishing is a division of Hachette Book Group, Inc.
The Grand Central Publishing name and logo is a trademark of Hachette Book Group, Inc.

The Hachette Speakers Bureau provides a wide range of authors for speaking events. To find out more, go to www.hachettespeakersbureau.com or call (866) 376-6591.

The publisher is not responsible for websites (or their content) that are not owned by the publisher.

ISBN 978-1-4555-1256-0 (pbk.)

*For anyone who's ever felt different
from everyone else.*

CONTENTS

Foreword

by Gwyneth Paltrow

I fell in love with Ross Mathews the first time I saw him. I was watching *The Tonight Show* one night, and he was covering the 2002 Winter Olympics in Salt Lake City. He made me laugh out loud—not an occurrence that happens to me regularly when I am watching most late-night television shows. His brand of humor was incredible, razor sharp, and yet sweet.

Our paths first crossed later that same year as I was headed into the famous *Vanity Fair* Oscar party. I can't remember exactly what happened, the order of things or what transpired, but he called out to me on the red carpet and I saw him, standing there on the press line, microphone in hand.

He looked harmless enough, like an adorable mix between a Cabbage Patch Kid and the Pillsbury Doughboy. Plus, I recognized him from that time I'd seen him on TV, so I decided to chat with him. Nothing has been the same since.

Within mere seconds, he asked if we could be best

friends—that I *do* remember. Coming from anyone else, it might've been creepy. But for some reason, without really thinking, I said yes.

I meant it.

He was so nervous during our first lunch date that he didn't even touch his food. On our second date he ate a bit more (the wine helped). After that dinner, we were off and running.

Throughout the past decade, we have been through a lot together, Ross and I—life's ups and downs, loves and deaths. I have watched his career take off, he has visited me in London, and each year on my birthday he sends me an erotic lesbian e-card. True story.

What started as a funny "Why Not?" has magically morphed into a legitimate bond. Sometimes in life, for reasons we don't always understand, we make these little connections. You see someone's face, they say something that makes you certain you are supposed to know them and you follow your heart. That's what happened with Rossy Pants and me. We may live oceans apart, but we are cut from the same cloth, to mix a metaphor.

Read this book. Trust me—you'll want to be his best friend, too.

Prologue

BALLOON DAY

Hello, dear reader! It's me, Ross Mathews from television! So now that we're best friends (oh, by the way, we *totally* just became best friends), you should know that I am possibly, just maybe a teeny bit *way* too excited for you to read my book. I'm so excited I just can't hide it. I'm about to lose control and I think I like it. Why? Because I've always dreamed of sharing my deepest, most top-secret thoughts with the world at large and now—OMG—it's finally happening.

Even as a little kid, I was the MVP of TMI, yearning to connect with people in any way I could. With that in mind, my favorite day of the school year wasn't Picture Day, Sloppy Joe Day, or even Bring Your Grandparents to School Day—all fine days in their own right. The day I looked forward to most was Balloon Day.

It occurs to me now that you might be confused, dear reader. Perhaps Balloon Day wasn't a national celebration that children in schools across the USA enjoyed. Who knows? Balloon Day may have been just a quaint, small-town phenomenon that my genius elementary school principal invented for the enjoyment of me and my fellow classmates every few years.

If this is, in fact, the first time you've ever heard of Balloon Day, I'm sorry that your childhood was so empty. Perhaps you might want to bring it up in your next therapy session as a possible reason for your fear of commitment. I'm just trying to help.

Balloon Day was awesome—that rare occasion that appealed to naive kindergarteners and jaded sixth graders alike. But as excited as all my classmates were for Balloon Day, my unapologetic gusto put them to shame. This event spoke to me. I loved not only the pageantry of it but the symbolism, as well, and my unbridled enthusiasm for it bordered on straight-up bonkers. But unlike the time I farted on the slide during recess in front of a group of popular fourth graders, none of my peers seemed to judge my boyhood balloon obsession too harshly, for they, too, loved Balloon Day.

Here's how the big day went down: On small pieces of paper no bigger than Tootsie Pop wrappers, my classmates and I would write our most heartfelt wishes, thoughts, and feelings. Each time my school celebrated Balloon Day, my personalized note was slightly different, but my penmanship was always immaculate. I took the process very seriously, treating it like a sacred communication between myself and the Great Unknown. In addition to my most private and profound thoughts, I'd also take the opportunity to humbly ask for a few actual gifts. Hey, couldn't hurt, right? You never know.

In second grade, I begged the Universe for a pony farm.

In fourth grade, I yearned for a pony farm and a doughnut factory. And finally, in sixth grade, I insisted on a pony farm, a doughnut factory, and, for reasons I didn't quite understand yet, TV's Jonathan Taylor Thomas. Each time, I would include my parents' home telephone number and end my message with, "If you find this note, please call me!"

Once the notes were written, the next and most important step of all was picking out our balloons. In the early days of kindergarten, I made the rookie mistake of being a gentleman, allowing all the girls in school to choose their balloon colors before I chose mine. It was a chivalrous gesture equivalent to putting my coat over a mud puddle for a darling damsel in distress, but it left me with a pathetically pitiful color palette of balloons from which to choose. An *orange* balloon? I don't think so. I'm a Spring, not a Fall, thank you very much.

I should have known better. Elementary school girls are as cutthroat as they are cute. Never again. By first grade, I was a seasoned pro. When it came to grabbing the best balloon of the bunch, it was survival of the fittest. With my kindergarten mistakes behind me, I now knew to shamelessly shove my way through the throng of annoying adolescent li'l ladies in order to reach the basket of uninflated balloons before those bitches could steal all the pink ones—my signature color, then and now.

After we selected our balloons, they were filled with helium and attached to our supersecret messages with a string by our gym teacher, a major hottie who looked like a cross between He-Man and Barbie's boyfriend Ken. Hubba hubba. Finally, the entire student body would march onto the grassy fields behind the gymnasium, with our balloons bobbing over our heads like multicolored thought bubbles.

"Hold on tight, kids," the teacher's aide would remind us. "Don't let go until we're all together."

What a well-meaning idiot. Bless her heart. Of course I was going to hold on to my balloon, dum-dum. Woman, puh-lease. We were all in this together, and if I let go early, I would ruin Balloon Day for everyone. That wasn't gonna happen, lady. Not on my watch. So I held on to that string with my fat little sausagelike prepubescent fingers with the same protective fervor with which I held my turkey and cheddar Lunchable. I'll admit, it was tempting to let go and give my message a head start, but I fought the urge.

"Okay, everybody," my principal shouted, causing my heart to beat even faster. I knew what was coming next, and it was by far, without a doubt, the absolute highlight of my entire year.

"Count it down with me, kids! One! Two! Three!"

In unison, we unclenched our hands, loosened our grips and released our balloons en masse into the air. It was, at that point in my young life, the most beautiful thing I had ever seen (short of TV's Jonathon Taylor Thomas). A sea of red, blue, yellow, green, orange, and pink balloons danced gracefully, intermingling and drifting higher and higher into the blue sky, each one carrying the precious cargo of children's wishes. We watched them, transfixed, until they shrank to the size of Skittles and eventually disappeared beyond the horizon.

In the days that followed, I would fantasize about my balloon's epic journey far away, into the world at large. Where would it end up? And more important, would whoever found it try to contact me? I would stay awake at night thinking about it, staring at the ceiling from beneath my *Jem and the Holograms* sheets, excited by the prospect of possibly hearing back from someone fabulous like a Parisian pen pal, or perhaps even a cool California kid whose uncle happened to work at Disneyland. Score!

To this day, I've yet to hear from anybody who ever found one of my airborne notes, but my fervent hope remains, and my parents' home telephone number is still the same. I'm not kidding. So keep your eyes peeled for any notes scribbled in impressive preteen penmanship and attached to decaying, decades-old pink balloons. They're most likely mine. If you do happen to find one, please feel free to call, especially if you're TV's Jonathan Taylor Thomas. I haven't seen you in years, JTT, but I bet you grew up to be hot. Short, but hot.

Oh, how I wish you could experience Balloon Day for yourself, dear reader, but you never will. Ever. Sadly, it's been outlawed. Why? Because as much as my classmates and I imagined our balloons ending up in a fairyland where wishes come true, they actually ended up in the delicate digestive systems of several endangered species. Major bummer.

Throughout the years, I have never forgotten the exhilaration and sense of connection I felt while sending my thoughts out into the Universe on the wings of an inflated pink balloon. It may sound like a lot of hot air, but in a way, I'd like to think of this book as the most personal message that I've ever sent out into the world. Even though

I didn't exactly tie it to a balloon and set it free, I'm so happy that it somehow landed with you.

Pretty warm and fuzzy stuff, huh? Well, before you break into a rousing chorus of "Kumbaya," let me warn you: shit's about to get real up in this biznatch.

This book, like my life, will be a bit of a roller coaster—you'll experience ups and downs, fits of laughter —and who knows, you might even throw up! So keep your arms and legs inside the ride at all times and, for goodness sake, stay seated until we come to a complete stop. And finally, if I'm going to reveal myself warts and all in this book, then I expect you to pay close attention. In order to make sure that you do just that, there is totally going to be a *Cosmo*-style quiz after the final chapter. For reals. I'm not joking. This is serious stuff. Feel free to take notes and perhaps grab your highlighter for the more important stuff.

Okay? Okay. Now, let's get started.

MAN UP!

Chapter One

MATHEWS VS. PHOBE

My dad taught me how to swear when I was just seven years old. We were driving home from the dump on a bumpy country road in his old Dodge pickup truck, me sitting on his lap steering while he worked the pedals, sipped a cold Schimdt's beer, and smoked a Marlboro. It was awesome. I couldn't have had a better swearing coach. My dad was the quintessential man's man—a mechanic and an avid hunter with a wonderfully naughty and raucous sense of humor.

"Shit," my dad muttered under his breath after hitting a bump in the dirt road, knocking the ashes from his lit cigarette onto the floor of the truck.

"Shit," I repeated, emulating him without thinking. I don't know why I said it. I just kind of repeated it mindlessly the way my grandmother's creepy parrots did. Immediately, I realized I had just said one of those bad words that I'd heard in the rap songs coming from my brother's room. I panicked.

Surprisingly, my dad thought it was hilarious. "Well, look at you," he chuckled. "Don't worry, it's okay. Say it again."

My eyes widened. Was this some sort of trick? But I decided to risk it. My squeaky voice shouted, "Shit!"

He laughed. I continued. "Shit shit shit shit shit shit!"

I was swearing like a grown-up and it felt fantastic. I don't know if it was just because of my swearing or the slight buzz he must have had after downing a few cold ones, but my dad was in hysterics. "Great! Now try saying 'fuck'!"

"Fuck!" God, this was fun.

"What other ones do you know, Rocky?" My dad always called me Rocky, I'm guessing because I must have reminded him of Sylvester Stallone.

I thought for a while. "Well, I know 'shit.' And 'fuck.' And 'poop.'..."

"Well, there are a bunch of other good ones, kiddo. I'll teach you. But you have to promise me that you'll only say them when you're with me."

"Forever?"

"Until you're older. When you become a man, then you can swear whenever the hell you want."

My dad must have known that a boy like me—sweet as pie and round as a cupcake—would most likely need some form of self-defense to get through life, so on that day he became my Mr. Miyagi of cussing. And to this day, thanks to him, even though I have the eyebrows and poise of a prize-winning beauty queen, I have the mouth of a road-hardened trucker.

He taught me that there is an art to swearing and, much like a chef mixes ingredients to build flavors, one can combine multiple obscenities for optimum effect. From then on, instead of a limp-fisted attempt at throwing down, I'd escape the wrath of bullies long enough to get away with a clever, "Go fuck yourself, you ball-fucking, shit-wiping, ass-cocking shit-fucker!"

You'd be shocked at how well that works. Much like martial arts or a credit card, however, one must use such unsavory language sparingly so as not to go overboard.

Even with my arsenal of swear words, it wasn't exactly easy growing up as me in Mount Vernon, Washington, a community too big to be considered a small town, but too small to be considered an actual city. Don't get me wrong: it's an absolutely lovely place full of kind-hearted people and an idyllic Main Street with brick sidewalks lining shops that sell charming items like windsocks and shotguns. With bragging rights that include exporting more tulips than Holland (put that in your wooden shoe and smoke it), Mount Vernon is also the hometown of some notable celebrities: actor James Caviezel, better known as Jesus from *The Passion of the Christ,* right-wing political commentator Glenn Beck, and...yours truly. Sing it with me, "One of these things is not like the other..."

Since I moved away in 1998 (about thirty seconds after graduating high school), an Olive Garden and a drive-through Starbucks have been built not far from where my mother still lives in the house where I was raised—a charming three-bedroom, two-bath rambler she and my father bought in 1978, a year before I came sashaying out of her uterus.

My mother worked as a bookkeeper at Mount Vernon High School, the very Mount Vernon High School where I once graced the stage as Henry Higgins in *My Fair Lady* (the lead role!) and sang in Synergy, the student jazz choir (very *Glee*, very ahead of its time). My mother is responsible for the delusional self-confidence that has made my career in the entertainment industry possible. Throughout my childhood, she was effusive with her compliments. Without fail, she would be the first to shower me with praise, always cheering, "You are *amazing*. You did *wonderfully*! You sing *beautifully*!"

Although she had the best of intentions, she may have been just a bit biased. Mother, I love you, but I've seen the VHS tapes of my performances, and although even Helen Keller could see my energetic passion, I was just okay.

If it's the job of older siblings to torture the younger ones, then my brother Eric—four years my senior—deserves Employee of the Decade. He was a total a-hole to me back then, only ever paying attention to me long enough to steal the remote or maniacally gloat over his Mario Bros. victory. Even the way he beat me up was evil. He would make a fist and extend the knuckle of his middle finger just a bit so it made a pointy spike, ensuring that the bruise on my arm would be a slightly darker purple in the middle. To this day, I rarely wear purple, which is a terrible shame, since it really makes my eyes sparkle.

I kind of hated him growing up, but we get along very well now. In retrospect, I totally understand why he picked on me. After all, until I showed up on the scene, he was the star of the show. And then, all of a sudden, here came this annoying Judy Garland version of a little brother and he was expected to just go along with it?

My brother's taunting aside, I was very blessed to be a

4

part of a family that embraced my uniqueness. My parents didn't bat an eye when I performed my rendition of the entire score to *Grease* in a backyard Broadway spectacular or when, instead of asking Santa for a Teenage Mutant Ninja Turtle for Christmas, I asked for a Cabbage Patch Kid...three years in a row...until I finally got one. His name was Randy, he had curly brown hair, and he was a Libra (just like me).

I was smart enough to know, though, that asking my parents for a Barbie doll was pushing it. So on my eighth birthday, after unwrapping yet *another* GI Joe, I improvised, leading to one of my greatest childhood discoveries: Play-Doh makes a fabulous miniwig in a pinch!

Adorned with perfectly sculpted heads of long, luxurious Play-Doh locks, my brigade of Joes was transformed into a bevy of Janes. With the addition of my one-of-a-kind haute couture toilet paper dresses, I single-handedly created Mount Vernon's tiniest drag revue ever. Not to brag, but my resourcefulness is rivaled only by *McGyver* (note to self: pitch *McGAYver* as a show idea to Bravo).

Eventually my makeshift, low-budget Barbies didn't cut it, so in order to afford the real deal, I had to get a job. I entered the workforce the summer before I turned thirteen and haven't looked back since. I loved working and felt very Christina Applegate in *Don't Tell Mom the Babysitter's Dead*. Kids, if you haven't seen this criminally underrated gem, do Uncle Ross a favor and Netflix it ASAP. You're welcome in advance.

Because Mount Vernon is a town rich with agriculture, pretty much any kid could get summer employment working in the fields. So, for my very first job, I ended up picking spinach for a local farm alongside half the population of my middle school.

Day after day I would haul my pasty, chubby, pre-pubescent body out into the fields, separating the male and female spinach plants to prevent pollination. I was like a "crop cockblocker."

Little known fact: male spinach plants have tiny yellow balls, and if you don't remove them, they will knock up the girl spinach plants...or something like that. To be honest, I don't really know—I barely know how it works with people—but they paid me $4.25 per hour to do it, so I didn't care.

Nearly two months into my career as a teen produce sexologist, my mind ripe with thoughts of a swelling bank account and fantasies of soon-to-be-purchased school clothes and glossy magazines of my very own, I was bitch-slapped by my first dose of outright homophobia.

Here's how it went down: Halfway through a long day of hunting for veggie testicles, my small group of spinach castrators and I were ready for a break. I stood up to stretch my back for a just a moment, when a shout echoed across the field. It was a phrase I'll never forget.

"Move your ass, faggot!"

I turned around to see my crew boss staring right at me, with a look of obvious contempt. He couldn't have been older than nineteen, but to me he was just a grown-up authority figure shouting what I still consider one of the worst words anyone could ever use. Sure, I'd heard that word before, but now that I was almost in my teens, I knew what it meant. I just stood there, dumbfounded. And then again, "Did you hear me, Ross? Move your ass, faggot!"

I'd like to say I took a "glamorous pause," but in truth, I was paralyzed, frozen in the hot sun. I didn't understand. I mean, he couldn't possibly be talking to me. *Me?* Not to the boy whose mother calls him, "Momma's most perfectest little angel face."

It was the first time in my twelve young years that I really felt the force field of my parents' love being shattered by the very real hatred and bigotry that exists in the world. I had absolutely no clue how to react.

I don't even remember that guy's name (let's just call him "Homer Phobe"), but I'll never forget his face. In fact, every once in a while I have a daydream about picking him out of a lineup like they do on reruns of *Law and Order: Special Victims Unit.* He steps toward the one-way mirror that protects my anonymity and Mariska Hargitay instructs him to repeat the phrase, "Move your ass, faggot."

I nod sheepishly, recognizing the subtleties in his hostile tone. "That's him."

He's then grilled by Christopher Meloni in a *very* dramatic prison cell scene. Next, after a commercial break, the jury erupts in spontaneous applause as I walk through the courtroom doors and take the stand to testify against him. My lawyer, Ryan Gosling (don't ask, it's my fantasy), and I masterfully recount the disturbing details and bring the truth to light. And as the jurors deliver their guilty verdict, my once-hardened assailant sheds his gruff exterior for the first time, comes to his senses, and silently mouths the words, *I'm sorry.*

Holding back tears with my head held high, I bravely commit an act of true empathy by looking Homer Phobe directly in the eye and slowly—*very* slowly—whispering, "I...Forgive...You," while Christopher Meloni nods in approval and Ryan Gosling gives me a lingering, victorious bear hug.

I'd like to say I handled it with that much class in real life, but I didn't. At all.

In actuality, I obsessed about what he had said for the rest of the workday. I didn't even enjoy my lunch, which is saying a lot because lunch was, and still is, my very favorite part of the day (well, tied with breakfast, dinner, and dessert). I was afraid, confused, and angry, but most of all, even at that age, I knew I just couldn't let it go.

When the whistle finally blew at the end of our shift, we did the usual routine—boarded the rented school buses and departed from the fields. I sat about five rows behind my bigoted crew boss, Homer Phobe, and stared directly at the back of his hateful head. My anxiety grew as each kid before me was dropped off in front of his or her home. When we reached my house, I clutched my yellow rubber boots with my sweaty palm and nervously trudged down the stairs of the bus. Just as the accordion door began to close behind me, I whipped around and slapped my hand against it, holding it ajar.

Before the bus driver could even ask me what I was doing, I lifted my shaking twelve-year-old hand, pointed my index finger at Homer Phobe and stated loudly, for all to hear, in a manner that would make my father beam with pride, "THAT FUCKING ASSHOLE CALLED ME A FAGGOT AND I'M NOT GONNA STAND FOR THIS SHIT! I QUIT!"

Without waiting a single second for Mr. Phobe's response, I let the bus door slam shut and ran for my ever-lovin' life.

As I burst through the front door of my house, my mom looked up from reading the paper and asked, "How was work, honey?"

Running past her into my bedroom, I caught a glimpse of myself in the mirror. Except for the smudge of dirt on my cheek, I looked the same as I did when I had left that morning—my round, freckled face darkened by the summer sun. But the change inside me was already evident. For the very first time in my life, I had made the decision to man up.

Smiling at my own reflection, I yelled back to my mother, "Spinach season is over."

I couldn't wait to tell my dad.

Chapter Two

LADIES' MAN

My romantic history with women is surprisingly vast. In my younger days, I was what my dad called a major "pussy magnet." But, when you think about it, my gift to attract the ladies is one of nature's cruelest jokes. Why give someone like *me* that power? That's like giving a butterfly a hammer. Sure, hammers are cool, but what in the hell is a butterfly supposed to do with it?

Still, I tried. Why? Because even though, deep down, I always knew I liked boys, dating girls was just what I thought was expected of me. I felt the same way about having to take algebra, even though I was certain I'd never use the Pythagorean Theorem when I grew up. But, sometimes the most important part of learning who you are is discovering who you aren't.

My first girlfriend was in fifth grade. Her name was Becky and she was one of the popular girls, which I assumed would immediately increase my social status by leaps and bounds on the playground. Plus, I liked her mom a lot because she had the same hairstyle as the mom on *Picket Fences*. I've always trusted a woman with a sensible bob.

Becky and I started going out the same day my friend Tara began dating this boy named Caleb. Just two preteen couples, trying to make a go of it in this crazy world...

In elementary school, "going out" meant that you spent recess together, stood next to each other in line for lunch, and shared a seat on the bus, so it was just about the right level of commitment for a ten-year-old me.

Becky asked me to be her boyfriend as we boarded the bus for a field trip to Wild Waves Water Park, an annual event at my elementary school and the one day every year that I dreaded the most. As an adult, I'm *still* not comfortable enough with my body to take my shirt off in front of strangers, but when you're ten years old and have man boobs that could fill a bikini top better than most of your prepubescent female classmates, water parks are your absolute worst nightmare. I usually spent the entire field trip making excuses to not remove my shirt. "Naw, I'm cool. You guys go ahead," I'd tell my friends while walking toward a pay phone. "I've gotta make a quick call."

Then I'd listen to the dial tone for twenty minutes or so while nervously planning my next move. I know what you must be thinking: if I didn't want to take my shirt off, why didn't I just go on the water slides with a T-shirt on? *Because the only thing more lame than being the guy with man boobs is being that guy who wears a T-shirt in a swimming pool.* It's like trying to cover a blemish with a neon green Band-Aid. I might as well have used an entire decade's allowance to hire a skywriter to scribble *Ross Mathews has man boobs!* high above the water park for all my normal-chested classmates to see.

But Becky, for some reason, didn't seem to mind my physical deformities, probably because she had one of her own: her hair was an absolute mess. It had always bugged me, even before we were boyfriend and girlfriend. For some reason I'll never understand, her mother—the same mother whose own hairstyle gave me such joy—gave Becky a perm and put in waaaay too much gel, so she always looked like she had a ball of uncooked Top Ramen noodles on her head.

Despite our flagrant flaws, I agreed to commit to Becky as my one and only true love. I was thrilled. I was in a full-fledged, real relationship! Just like the people on TV—*very* Uncle Jesse and Aunt Becky on *Full House.*

Of course, I understood that being in a mature relationship wouldn't be easy. Going forward, compromise would be essential. I knew that if she wanted the red crayon, she could have it...just as soon as I was done with it. And if there was only one empty swing left on the playground, she could push me until the end of recess. That's how compromise works.

Unfortunately, Becky and I never made it to that stage of our relationship. On the very same day our romance began, it came to a sudden and screeching halt. During the bus ride home, her swimsuit still damp from Wild Waves fun, things got...complicated. After huddling with her friends in the seat next to ours, my main squeeze Becky turned to me and declared, "I'm breaking up with you. You're going out with Tara now."

Her declaration hit me like a ton of Legos. "What?" I

stammered. "I am? But I thought Tara just started going out with Caleb."

"They *were* going out, but I just traded you for him. Go sit next to your new girlfriend."

What a nasty bitch, right? She *traded* me?!? What am I, a lousy homemade bologna sandwich you try to swap for a store-bought Jell-O chocolate puddin' snack?

In hindsight, I wish I would've told her to take her crunchy hair and get bent, but I didn't. I just went along with it, which was totally unfair because my new girlfriend Tara wore tan corduroys and smelled like Thousand Island dressing. Luckily for me, though, my new relationship with Tara was even shorter than my previous one with Becky. Not two minutes after I sat down next to her, both of us glaring at our exes-turned-happy-couple, Tara added insult to injury when she huffed, "This isn't working. I think we should see other people."

Women—am I right?

I was left emotionally scarred and for years refused to get close to any woman other than Little Debbie or Debbie Gibson. It wasn't until I entered the seventh grade and turned thirteen that I met the girl of my dreams, a fabulous young lady so full of verve and panache that one couldn't help but compare her to a young Liza Minnelli. She simply had to be mine!

Maria was a spicy senorita whose last name, ironically enough, was the same as my favorite brand of salsa. She had silky-smooth dark hair, big brown eyes, and ruby red lips. She was dainty and delicate, resembling one of Marie Osmond's signature collectible porcelain dolls from QVC. That is, until your eyes strayed from her angelic face and down to her prematurely large breasts. Seriously, this fourteen-year-old girl had the jugs of a middle-aged cocktail waitress.

Despite her Double D-lightful endowments, we started dating immediately. This consisted mainly of talking on the telephone for hours each and every night, about anything and everything—from drama in our middle school to drama in the Middle East. On the weekends, we would go to the movies together, holding hands in the dark and reaching various make-out milestones while watching classics like *Aladdin* (our first kiss), *The Bodyguard* (our first under-the-sweater action) and the Elizabeth Perkins existential gem, *Indian Summer* (during which we engaged in something I would later learn from my older brother was affectionately referred to as "finger banging").

No, your eyes are not deceiving you. I did indeed take a "hands-on" approach with precious Maria. You may be surprised to learn that I was particularly adept at manual stimulation. I was so talented, in fact, that Maria and I were kicked out of *Indian Summer* because of her audible pleasure. Yeah, I'm *that* good! I wish I knew how to share my technique with you all, but I just can't put my finger on it.

It's a well-known fact that girls mature faster than boys. And when you consider that Maria was a full year older than me, you essentially have the equivalent of Samantha from *Sex and the City* dating Doogie Howser. Yep, Maria was a fourteen-year-old cougar and, like her feline namesake, she was hungry for raw meat. My raw meat. And by "raw meat," I mean my wiener.

She was downright insatiable, and I was on 24/7 crotch

watch, constantly swatting her hand away from my private area and finding increasingly creative excuses not to go any further. "Oh Maria, I so very much wish I could do that with you," I'd try to cover, as my panicked voice built in both speed and pitch. "But I simply must leave right this very moment, because it's Thursday and Thursday is the day I read the latest issue of *Reader's Digest* to the lonely old senior citizens at the retirement center and I have to grab some hot tea with honey because they love it when I do the voices, but I've had this tickle in my throat all day and I really don't want to let them down because they're so very old and frail and I'm all they have in this horrible world and they could die at any moment. So, as flattered as I am, Maria, by your incessant clawing at *that* area, I've really got to *get the fuck outta here!!!*"

Apart from lying to her sexually frustrated face to avoid any physical contact beyond my fancy fingerwork, I was an absolute perfect boyfriend. I was so attentive to my number one gal, in fact, that every single night I called KBRC, Mount Vernon's local AM radio station, and requested our song.

I'd turn up the volume and hug my radio when I finally heard the DJ croon, "There's nothing sweeter than puppy love, is there? This one goes out from Rossy-Wossy to his little burrito of love, Maria. Here's Whitney Houston with 'I Will Always Love You'..."

Maria was cruelly ripped from my life when her family decided to leave our small town for the bright lights of Las Vegas. Suddenly our song went from "I Will Always Love You" to Roxette's "It Must Have Been Love." God, teen love can be painful.

But, alas, life goes on, and soon I was ready to love again. I briefly dated a girl named Danni who had perfect eyebrows and lived in the trailer park behind my middle school. Her parents had a *Kama Sutra* book we secretly flipped through before making out. We found the exotically erotic images arousing, confusing, and intriguing at the same time, much like how I feel now while watching the Food Network. I ran into Danni recently at Wilsons Leather the last time I visited my hometown. She was the proud mother of three great kids and two still-amazing eyebrows.

My most serious relationship with a woman was in high school. We got to know each other in those steamy hotbeds of sordid teen romance known as Drama Class, Jazz Choir, and Debate Club. Carrie was gorgeous: Long strawberry-blonde hair, milky-white skin, adorable freckles, and an ample bosom.

She was assigned the job as my official dresser throughout my award-worthy portrayal of Henry Higgins in the Mount Vernon High School production of *My Fair Lady*, helping me in and out of my costumes (which is *almost* as sensual as it sounds). Once Carrie saw me in my polka-dot boxer shorts and top hat during intermission, she was hooked. So was I. After all, much like Barbra Streisand, she was a triple threat: smart, funny, and talented. In a show-biz minute we became the very best of friends, spending nearly every waking moment together. Eventually, we shared the ultimate bonding experience between a man and a woman: a makeover!

Although I adored Carrie's long flowing hair, it was un-deniably dry and suffering from unfortunate split ends. It simply wasn't an accurate reflection of her bouncy, lustrous personality. Frankly, she deserved better hair, and I was just the man who could help! So, not unlike the *My Fair Lady* character I so magically portrayed onstage, I convinced my very own real-life Eliza Doolittle to cut that unsightly haystack into a sleek, sophisticated bob.

I offered reassuring looks and approving nods as she sat in the pleather chair of the beauty salon conveniently located in the strip mall between Thrifty Foods and Little Caesar's Pizza. As I describe this, please imagine the song "Pretty Woman" playing over alternating shots of scissors snipping and long strands of bone-dry, beige hair floating down to the linoleum floor. When the skilled-but-affordable stylist finally swiveled Carrie around to face me and whipped the protective black nylon smock from her alabaster neck, I was in love. Her new 'do looked so healthy and strong! There, staring up at me was the stunningly perfect combination of Posh and Ginger Spice!! I squealed with delight, clapping my hands and enthusiastically jumping up and down while screaming, *"So pretty!!!"*

Talk about turned on. Her new look knocked me for such a loop that we made out that night. A lot.

In hindsight, and now with some life experience under my belt, making out with a girl is much like making out with a guy—except softer and much less enjoyable. It's not that I wasn't into it, per se, but I approached it more like a lab experiment than a hormone-fueled sexcapade. It was as if I were studying rocks instead of getting my rocks off. Lighting a Bunsen burner as opposed to burning with desire. I was merely trying to pass the class, not trying to tap that ass.

(Honesty moment: The previous paragraph contains absolutely everything I know about both women *and* science.)

My special friendship with Carrie quickly progressed, and before I knew it, we were officially boyfriend and girlfriend. I found committed relationships in high school to be very different than when I had gone out with girls in grade school. Back then, simply sitting on the bus and holding hands was enough to satisfy my partner. But in the eleventh grade, the stakes were much higher. I knew what was coming and I was terrified.

It happened at her house. Allow me to set the scene: it was just the two of us, lying on her bed, watching the ultimate aphrodisiac of animated movies, the film that no doubt has led many innocent teens to carelessly fling themselves into the fiery pit of passion: *The Lion King*.

I was somewhat taken aback when, during the most dramatic scene in the movie, the one in which Simba's father is (spoiler alert!) brutally killed, Carrie got up and left the room. I thought about hitting Pause on the VCR when I heard the shower go on in the adjacent bathroom. I wasn't overly concerned. After all, Carrie and I had watched this movie like seven times together before, so it's not like she was missing anything. Besides, that scene always made me feel dirty, too. She probably couldn't bear to watch that heart-wrenching moment yet again. *I hope she takes her time in there,* I thought to myself, *you know—loofah, exfoliate, deep-condition...*

I was very in tune with Carrie. Yes, we were like one that way, always on the same page. After all, this was the girl who sang *Rent* in the car with me, never struggling to achieve flawless, Broadway-caliber harmonies. She could always finish my sentences and I would always finish her nachos. Utter synchronicity.

Five minutes and one Elton John ballad sung by African wildlife later, Carrie emerged from the bathroom in a cloud of Pantene-scented steam. She was wearing nothing but a towel and a sultry, vixen-like stare.

(INSERT RECORD-SCRATCH SOUND EFFECT HERE.)

I was certainly no expert in lovemaking, but I'd seen enough soap operas to know what it meant when a girl entered a room wearing simply a towel surrounded by steam. Oh God. It was happening. I tried to stall. "Do you, uh, want to finish the movie?"

She slowly shook her damp head. "No," she purred, staring at me like a starving jungle cat leering at a succulent pork chop.

Oh. Dear. God. It was happening. It was *really* happening. Every last instinct told me to just push Play on the remote control and continue watching the movie in one last-ditch effort to extinguish her burning desires. But before I could make my move, she made hers: she dropped the towel.

Oh dear God in heaven! Here I was, *The Lion King* on Pause and a naked woman—a natural blonde, by the way—standing before me. The law of the jungle is eat or be eaten, so I made a snap judgment and thought to myself, *Hakuna Matata!*

I committed fully. Gosh darn it, if I was going to do this I was going to do it right! So after making out for a bit, I bravely shimmied "down South" until I was face-to-face...with a vagina. It was a normal-looking vagina, I guess. Like a sideways smile—or a frown—depending on how you looked at it. There was no turning back now.

Three...two...one...I closed my eyes and went at it like a fat kid in a pie-eating contest at the county fair.

It was fascinating. It was kind of like trying to eat a plastic toy ice cream cone—you can lick and lick forever, but it just won't go away.

Eventually I stopped to take a breather and get another good look at it. It was...unreal. It was bizarre. I had so many questions. I kept trying to figure out how it worked. *What part of this thing does the peeing?* There was simply so much going on! I mean, this was no Barbie doll crotch—this was the real deal—and I found myself wishing it came with an instruction manual. It was much too confusing. I didn't like it. I didn't want to do it anymore.

Eventually, she noticed that I'd stopped and sweetly asked me, "Ross, are you okay?"

I'm not sure how to describe my response. It didn't consist of words, just a guttural whimper of resigned defeat. "Ehhh-huhhhhhgggggghhhhh."

Needless to say, that kind of killed the mood. I felt horrible, like I had just somehow dissed her vagina. Don't get me wrong, it was a pretty part of a pretty girl, but I was pretty sure that it wasn't for me. And it was pretty clear that I wasn't the boy for her. Yes, I could help give her a hot new hairstyle, but I could never help give her an orgasm. She deserved a guy who would dive right in with wild abandon and passionately ravage her lovely lady parts, not study them like a periodic table. Although we broke up shortly thereafter, Carrie and I still remained good friends.

I don't regret what we did that night. I think I heard Oprah say once that we should all do something every day that scares us. I believe that, too, and I'm all the better for it. But what I gained in self-respect that day didn't come without a price. You see, I haven't been able to watch *The Lion King* ever since. For some reason, it just leaves a bad taste in my mouth.

God bless all these amazing ladies: Becky, Tara, Maria, Danni, and, most of all, darling Carrie. These wonderful women sacrificed very intimate parts of themselves—some more intimate than others—so that I could one day discover something very intimate about myself: I am a (spoiler alert!) raging homosexual.

Thanks, girlfriends!

Chapter Three

VOICE MALE?

If, like me, you happen to possess a voice that could be mistaken for a clown on helium, here are a few professions you may want to avoid: Monster truck rally announcer, Morgan Freeman impersonator, and, most definitely, on-air television personality. I cannot tell you how many times I've been given this helpful advice throughout my life and career. Luckily for me, I've also heard another voice in my head squeaking even louder, *Don't listen to those Negative Nancys!*

The first thing any good acting teacher, life coach, or spiritual guru worth their weight in tofu will tell you is, "Find your voice."

That's excellent guidance, but believe it or not, there was actually a time when I wished I could've lost mine.

When I was a little kid, my voice was no different than any other child's my age—boy or girl. Creepy ghost stories and hilarious poop jokes alike were told in pleasantly melodic, gender-neutral tones. Somewhere around the age of nine, however, things shifted and I became all too aware that I sounded more like a Jane than a Dick.

As my peers and I entered adolescence, life was becoming more and more exciting. Thankfully, along with acne and growing pains also came new freedoms. Suddenly, my friends and I could go to grown-up PG-13 movies without our parents and pick out school clothes of our very own.

Most thrilling of all, our bodies were developing just like we were promised they would in health class. *Well hello, hair down there!* Every day, our young lives were in a constant state of change. For me, however, it seemed like the only thing not changing was my voice.

While the other boys were beginning to sound like truck drivers with emphysema, everything coming out of my mouth sounded uncannily like a perky actress in a tampon commercial. I kept assuring myself, "Don't fret, Ross! Your voice will change soon! You're just a late bloomer!"

Yes, I was optimistic. I knew there was still time. After all, both my dad and my brother had low, booming voices. Gruff, manly tones ran in the Mathews family! Heck, even my mom's sweet voice was more butch than mine. I came from good genes, dammit! I was sure it would be no time at all before I sounded like a genuine grown-up gentleman.

But just like the sequel to *Titanic* that I've always hoped they'd make (where it turns out that Leonardo DiCaprio didn't really [spoiler alert!] freeze to death, and he and Kate Winslet enjoy a long happy life making sexy babies and living off the millions they made from selling the Heart of the Ocean necklace), it just wasn't meant to be.

Don't get me wrong—it's not like I woke up every morning desperately hoping my voice had changed. I knew I sounded different from the other boys, but I guess I was so used to it that it didn't seem weird to me. My voice was just my voice. Like JLo's ass or Mariah's ego, it was just a huge part of me. It wasn't until my classmates started making fun of it that it became an issue. I was a pretty confident kid, but their merciless mockery really started to hurt my feelings.

I tried to reason with my cruel peers, pleading with them to stop. "Come on, you guys. Words can hurt and you know that's not nice. Maybe you're only picking on me because you're unhappy with yourself? It's like last week's episode of *Blossom* where Joey made fun of her for being brainy, but once he looked within, he realized that he just felt inferior because he'd failed his math test. Oh my God, did you guys see it? Joey Lawrence is *such* an amazing actor, don't you think? You guys...?"

Obviously, this weak attempt to silence my hateful hecklers and/or completely change the subject made them tease me even more (in their defense, just reading it right now kinda makes me want to give myself a wedgie). I wish that I could have gotten in touch with my rage and let it fuel me like the Incredible Hulk, mutating into something fabulously dangerous, part Elpheba from *Wicked* on steroids and part Faye Dunaway in *Mommie Dearest.*

My superhero name would be The Shrill, and my costume would be made out of unforgiving spandex—man boobs be damned! It would be a fashion risk I'd be willing to take for the greater good.

My signature superhero colors would be head-to-toe pastels. Enraged by injustice and insensitivity, I'd unleash my superpowers with such fury that all bullying, taunting, and teasing—directed not only at me but toward everyone all over the planet—would immediately come to a screeching halt! In defense of us all, I would scale the highest mountain with superhuman strength and, in the divinely unique voice God gave me, I'd boldly bellow that infamous quote from Ms. Dunaway in *Mommie Dearest*, erupting with the unbridled fury of Joan Crawford: "*Don't fuck with me, fellas!*"

But I never did fight back. And if I had managed to somehow harness all that wild ferociousness and retaliate against my misguided aggressors, chances are that no one would have taken me seriously anyway. I mean, let's face it, I probably would've sounded about as badass as everyone's favorite aunt asking them to get their elbows off the dinner table.

But do you know what bugged me even more than my bullies' nasty intentions? The crappy caliber of their insults. Seriously, these half-assed attempts were just stupid. Take, for instance, when the biggest, dumbest bully in school hurled what he thought was a brilliant verbal assault and actually called me a "girl talker." As in, "Hey, what's wrong with your voice, Girl Talker? You talk like a girl! Haw haw haw!"

Girl Talker? Ouch. Really, dude? Come on, now. I may sound like a girl, but even I can do better than that. So here, for your enjoyment, are a few well-designed disses aimed at my ladylike larynx:

- My voice is so high-pitched, only gay dogs can hear it.
- Even Richard Simmons thinks I should butch it up.
- My voice is the only thing Don't Ask, Don't Tell still applies to.

- You'd think I'd like vaginas, since most people with my voice have one.
- Equal parts my voice and Fran Drescher's voice are how doctors cure those four-hour Viagra erections men are warned about.
- The recorded version of this book—read by me—is so torturous that it could replace water boarding.
- My drag name would be Ross Mathews.

Learning to laugh at myself before anyone else can has allowed me to not only stop hating my voice, but actually love it. It's an age-old tale of self-acceptance. One needn't look any further than classic literature for countless examples. Can't think of any? Hello, dum-dum! Haven't you read *Rudolph the Red-Nosed Reindeer*? Guess what—it happens to be a song, too, and a great stop-motion movie that, for some reason, they only show like once a year.

Without ruining the ending, the gist is that he's a gay reindeer who can't afford a nose job, but he becomes a superstar in the end. It's all very inspirational.

It turns out that, just like Rudolph, what I initially considered to be such a negative is, in fact, the very thing that has made me stand out. Not to sound preachy, but accepting my voice has given me the confidence I've needed to pursue my dreams. And just like Seal rocks his facial scars, Cindy Crawford works her mole, and Barbra Streisand wins every race by a nose, I hope you're inspired to make the most of your possibly less-than-perfect trademark, too.

(God, do me a quick favor and just reread that last paragraph, will you? I'm superwise, like one of those ancient wizards with a long white beard and a pointy hat from a medieval fantasy-adventure movie! God, those robes look comfy, like a magical muumuu!)

One day I just decided to face the facts. Unless I start gargling with lighter fluid or smoking three packs of filterless cigarettes a day, my voice is never going to change. And you know what? I'm fine with that. Really. I've totally come to terms with it. I think I sound perfectly lovely. Plus, there have been times in everyday life when having a voice like mine has actually paid off in surprising and fantastic ways.

For instance, there was this one time when my car was stuck in the repair shop for an entire week. When I called to see if it was ready to be picked up, the macho mechanic got straight to the point. "Sorry, but it's not gonna be ready for a few more days."

Without thinking, I moaned, "Oh no! I need it back really, *really* bad!"

Suddenly, his hard tone softened. "Well, little lady, it sounds like you're in quite a pickle."

If only he knew that this "little lady" was packing a pickle of his own! But, what the hell, I decided to just go with it. "Well, I guess I am! Are you *sure* there isn't *anything* you could do?"

Eww! It was all so cheesy and sounded way too much like dialogue from the beginning of a low-budget porno movie, but he was swayed by my sweet talk and totally took the bait. "Well, I suppose I could pull a few strings, but only for you, honey. I'll have her ready for you by five o'clock this evening."

Oh my God, I couldn't believe it! My high-pitched voice was totally making this mechanic pitch a tent! Here I was a big-bellied boy, but he was convinced he was flirting with a busty blonde bimbo. When I picked my car up at five o'clock, I was gonna surprise him with a five o'clock shadow. Whatever! All that mattered was that I was getting my car back early!

At five o'clock on the dot, I arrived at the shop and declared with a triumphant and toothy smile, *"Yoo-hoo!!! I'm here for my car!!!"*

I don't know if the mechanic even put two and two together, the poor thing. He just kind of stared at me blankly, wondering why someone other than the pretty lady of his dreams was picking up the car. But ignorance is bliss, right? At the end of the day, I had my car back early and he'd had his fantasy of the damsel in distress. It was a win-win.

But trust me: when it comes to my voice, this kind of happy ending is very rare. Usually, I don't even realize that I sound different from any other guy until I'm rudely snapped into reality by well-meaning (and sometimes not-so-well-meaning) strangers.

You see, it isn't always easy living in a world like ours with a voice like mine. I have to brace myself for those inevitable, awkward moments that accompany situations like these: every time I place an order in a fast food drive-through ("Pull up to the second window, ma'am"), whenever I meet brutally honest and annoyingly curious young children ("Hey mister, why do you sound like a lady?"), and every time I answer a telephone ("May I please speak to the man of the house?").

Oh, please, don't *even* get me started with the telephone! I can honestly say that I've never been called "Sir" by a stranger on the other end of a phone in my entire life. *Ever.* One of the very worst experiences had to be the time I called my cell phone carrier to cancel my plan. I won't divulge the name of the specific company right here in my book because that would be downright tacky. Instead, I will be classy and refrain. I will, however, simply say that it rhymes with *splint* and is another word for a short burst of fast running.

Despite giving them all the information they demanded— address, Social Security number, mother's maiden name, favorite Broadway musical (*Bye Bye Birdie*, bee-tee- dubs)—the snooty operator refused to close my account because she was convinced I was not only a woman but one with ulterior motives.

She told me, in a bitchy Southern accent, "Ma'am, we do not believe that you are Ross Mathews. We believe that you are, in fact, Mr. Mathews's vindictive ex-girlfriend who is trying to cancel his account to get back at him for whatever reason."

Oh no she didn't! My face was red-hot as I white- knuckled my baby-pink phone. I was dead set on proving to her that I was, in fact, 100 percent Grade A man meat. I cleared my throat, clenched my teeth and, in the low- est, butchest register I could muster, channeled my inner Clint Eastwood and snarled, "I can assure you with ab- solute certainty, this is not Ross Mathews's ex-girlfriend. And furthermore—"

She interrupted me, "Ma'am, I'm gonna have to ask you to calm down."

Well, that didn't work. Try as I may, I was still coming across more Debbie Harry than Dirty Harry. So, instead of completing what should have been a very simple phone transaction, I had to drop everything and *Sprint* (cough, cough) over to their closest store location to cancel my account in person. Not only was it a total inconvenience, but it was also completely embarrassing. Thank God there was a sale at the Old Navy next door, so it wasn't a total loss. I found a wonderful teal-blue cardigan on the clearance rack that I still wear to this very day.

As bad as that experience was, what happened to me on stage a few years later was even worse. I was performing at a casino in Lake Tahoe as the opening act for my beloved Chelsea Handler. The audience seemed to be enjoying themselves, mostly because, let's face it, they were delightfully drunk off their asses. One particularly shit-faced gentleman in the front row interrupted my act and loudly slurred to his date while pointing right at me, "Hey! Issit juz me, or does she kinda look like a guy?"

Yep, that happened. And *everyone* heard it. Then the entire crowd—hundreds of complete strangers—burst into hysterical laughter. And you know what? So did I. I mean, come on, that's funny on so many levels. As I stood there giggling like a schoolgirl along with the audience, I knew I had just marked a major milestone. I had struggled to accept my voice for my entire life, and now I knew without a doubt, through highs and lows (okay, mostly highs), that I had fully embraced my voice once and for all.

It turns out, when it comes to my voice, I'm kinda like a

twist on the famous slogan from that old deodorant commercial. Remember? "Strong enough for a man, but made for a woman."

Except in my case, I'm strong enough *as* a man to sound *like* a woman.

Chapter Four

ROSS THE INTERN 1: TV AND ME

I've had a lifelong love affair with television. In fact, I was practically raised on TV, always making a beeline home from school straight to the living room couch, with just a quick pit stop at the fridge to load up on snacks. Countless hours were spent in motionless, glazed-over, catatonic bliss. Admittedly, there were certain strange side effects from all that time spent in front of the tube. I would make up and sing snappy jingles under my breath for every item on the school lunch menu. For example, to the tune of *The Flintstones*: "Fish sticks! Get your fish sticks! Yummy tummy gonna eat you...I'm gonna eat you...I'm gonna make you miiiine!"

Also unsettling, I began to tell time by my television schedule as opposed to a clock. "Okay," I'd tell my friends, "I can come hang out at your house from *Who's The Boss?* until half past *America's Funniest Home Videos*, but I have to be home by *Rescue 911*."

My obsession got even worse when I got a TV of my very own, a 10-inch color Panasonic TV I bought at a garage sale in a trailer park not far from my parents' house. I remember thinking it was odd that it was called a garage sale when none of the trailer homes actually had garages, but no matter. And once I saw that little black-and-tan box shining like a beacon in the midst of old baby clothes and dusty copies of *National Geographic*, I didn't care anymore about semantics. I was sold!

It was 1989. I paid $11 for her and, if you ask me, she was worth every single penny. We bonded instantly and I named her Jessica—Jessica Spano Mathews.

You get major friend points if you noticed that she was named after the overachieving, curly-haired, caffeine-pill-addicted Jessie Spano from one of the greatest TV shows of all time, *Saved by the Bell*.

No lie: I have seen every episode of *Saved by the Bell* at least four times. I dare you to challenge me to a *SBTB* trivia contest. Go ahead…you'll lose. What was Screech's parents' dog's name? Elvis. Totally true. He was a hound dog. Look it up, loser. What does the A.C. in A.C. Slater stand for? Albert Clifford. Boom, mothafucka!

Right about now you probably understand why my best friend growing up was a TV. My best friend, Jessica, didn't have an antenna, so try as she might, her reception wasn't always as strong as it could have been. So I accessorized her with the cutest little homemade tinfoil hat. Fashion *and* function—she was a looker!

Now, I'm not an old man or anything, but you whippersnappers don't know what it used to be like back in the day. I mean, before cellular telephones and before Sandy Bullock was an Oscar winner, there was a time when most people didn't have cable. It was a completely different world! Back then, there were only a few channels, and if you didn't like what was on TV, you had to—get this—stand up, walk all the way across the room, and physically change the channel on the TV yourself.

Good cardio, yes. But a major pain in the butt.

Just think about that for a minute, you spoiled brats with your remote controls and your five thousand high-definition channels. When I grew up, we lived like pilgrims. And it gets worse! Because I lived in farm country, Jessica picked up only two channels. *Two!*

Even worse: of the two channels Jessica picked up, one was Spanish-language and the other played episodes of *Saved by the Bell* only on Saturday mornings. Every other day, they played nothing but random shows in syndication from at least ten years earlier. So instead of keeping up with what my peers were watching, I was limited to viewing re-runs of *Taxi*, *M*A*S*H*, *WKRP in Cincinnati*, *Three's Company*, and the like. What I thought was cool in 1989 had long since reached its expiration date, so I was always making outdated pop culture references in my fifth-grade classroom like "That is *so* Jack Tripper!" to the blank stares of my classmates.

It was the effect of this kind of humiliation that finally persuaded my parents to allow the miracle of cable into our household.

Amen! I remember the moment we got connected as if it were yesterday. I swear, up until that point, it felt like I had been raised in the woods by unicorns. But now, the Mathews family had finally caught up with the rest of the civilized world, and I had work to do! Hello, the *Fresh Prince of Bel Air* theme song wasn't gonna memorize itself! And who was this Urkel character?!? Nerd alert—this guy's hilarious!

Cable opened up a brand-new world to me that I had never even ventured to imagine. It was everything and more. Even Jessica looked happier, although I could detect a tinge of jealousy on weekday afternoons when I'd sit down to spend an hour with the woman who, until her cruel departure from the airwaves, held the title of My Longest Running Relationship: Oprah.

OMO: Oh My Oprah! I love her andIdon'tevencare. I love her thin, I love her big, but I prefer her big because the more Oprah, the better, right? I can't get enough!

Oprah was like a hot air balloon that would whisk me away. Thanks to her talk show, I got to meet celebrities, travel the world, and see things I never would've seen in Mount Vernon. Oprah was the shining jewel in the crown of the golden era of daytime TV. Nobody did it like Lady O, but I consider all the talk show hosts of the 1990s to be huge influences: Sally Jesse Raphael, Montel Williams, Rikki Lake, Geraldo Rivera, Maury Povich, Phil Donahue, Gordon Elliott, Leeza Gibbons, Jerry Springer...hell, even Jenny Jones!

These talk show hosts enthralled me even more than their salacious guests, and I wanted nothing more than to be just like them. I remember running to turn the volume down just before commercial breaks so I could be the one to say, "What will Michelle do when she finds out her incarcerated boyfriend is, in fact, really her brother? And he...is now a she! We'll be right back!"

My mother, bless her heart, especially got a kick out of this. It was our ritual to watch *Live! with Regis and Kathie Lee* together every morning during our summer vacations. There was something special about watching that daytime dynamic duo. They were better than all the others and second only to Oprah. It may sound odd, but my life's purpose suddenly became crystal clear one morning while watching Reege 'n' Kath interviewing the star du jour. Seated on the couch next to my mother, I had an epiphany. *This is it,* I thought to myself. *This is what I'm meant to do with my life. I was put on this planet to make casual conversation with celebrities over a morning cup of coffee while America watches.*

But, of course, it was deeper than that. I liked the way the old guy and the wacky red-headed gal made me feel. I liked how happy they made my mom. They were an escape, a glimpse into a world far away from Mount Vernon, an excuse to smile for an hour at a time. I wanted to do that for people, too.

From that moment forward, I had no other choice. My mind was made up. I simply *had* to become a talk show host or my life would be a complete failure. I distinctly remember, whenever an adult would ask me, "What do you want to be when you grow up?" I'd always respond, "A television talk show host!"

I was ten and I already *knew* it was my destiny to be on TV. I mean, seriously though, what other career choices did I have? Can you picture me as, like, a cop? With, like, a uniform and a real weapon and everything? I'd be all like, "Stop, bad guy! Wait, get back here! Please?!? Come on, I'm serious. For reals. That's, like, totally against the law. Don't even make me use this gun! Pretty please?!?"

It was obvious. I *had* to be on TV.

Of course, there is no clear path to becoming a talk show host. I mean, you never see ads on craigslist that read, "Talk Show Host Wanted: Earn millions while fulfilling your dreams and riding in limousines."

So at eighteen years old, armed with only the $500 I had earned working the entire summer, I hightailed it to the Hollywood-adjacent University of La Verne. I pulled away from my parents' house and drove down Interstate 5 with a head full of dreams and a tank full of gas in my blue Ford Tempo.

When I arrived in California, my car nearly scraped the ground under the weight of all my worldly possessions. My favorite items, in no particular order, were my VHS copy of *Steel Magnolias*, the complete boxed set of the *Little House on the Prairie* books, my framed autographed photo of Tiffani-Amber Thiessen, and, last but by no means least, my beloved TV Jessica.

College life agreed with me. To be honest, I spent the majority of my freshman year of college gossiping in the dorms with my newly acquired besties while snacking on Sour Skittles, listening to Christina Aguilera and Britney Spears albums on repeat and making regular late-night runs to In-N-Out for a Double-Double with extra sauce and grilled onions. Life was so good. I couldn't see my feet, but life was good. I was shopping in the husky department, but life was good.

The *best* part about going to college, you guys? Two words: dining hall. Now, I know what you kids are probably thinking. "Ross, yuck! The food in the dining hall is, like, totally gross, dude!"

But let me explain something to you young'uns. I'm telling you this as a grown-up with life experience. Food is like sex. If you're getting it on a regular basis *for free*, even if it's bad, be grateful, 'cuz, trust me, you're gonna miss it when it's gone. These valuable life lessons come at no extra charge with the purchase of this book. You're welcome.

College seemed to fly by with more speed than I'd gobble down those In-N-Out Double-Doubles. In a hot second, it was suddenly senior year and I was on the brink of graduating and entering the workforce. Granted, I had learned a lot after four years of college classes, but can I let you in on a little secret? I had no real skills. When it came to the real world, I only knew two things for certain: one, always wear sandals in a public shower; and two, it is indeed possible to memorize every single line in the movie *Pretty Woman*. "You work on commission, right? Big mistake, big, huge..."

This realization hit me one day in my dorm room, knee-deep in empty BBQ Baked Lay bags and waaaay too caught up in the fourth and, sadly, final season of *Felicity*. Grown-up life was quickly approaching and, until I became a famous talk show host, I had no idea how I was going to make a living.

I imagined myself as a college graduate at the unemployment office being asked to list my professional capabilities.

"I can, umm, tell you if a spinach plant is a boy or a girl. And I like to watch movies, and if a movie is really bad I'll, like, say it and be all, like, 'That movie wasn't very good.' Also, I can name all the members of 'N Sync, the Back-street Boys, and New Kids on the Block. I can even list all the guys in 98 Degrees, and that's really impressive because *no one* knows all their names. Most people only know Nick Lachey because he's dating Jessica Simpson. I love them! Cutest couple of all time! They're gonna be together forever and ever and ever!"

I was *so* screwed. I mean, even if I did get a job after graduation, what kind of job would help me get any closer to becoming a talk show host? If I was ever going to give it a real shot, I knew this was the time for me to do it. But I also knew that opportunity wasn't just going to knock on my door. Or was it?

A few days later, my friend Melanie dropped by my dorm room to catch up on what we had each done during our summer breaks. I went first, regaling her with wild stories about my time spent up in Washington State staying at my parents' house. Pretty riveting stuff. Then it was her turn.

"Oh, I just..." Melanie really took her time, drawing out her story for dramatic effect "...you know, interned at *The Tonight Show with Jay Leno.*"

I almost slapped her in her pretty little face right then and there.

"*You what?!?* How? Why? What was it like? Did you meet him? Holy crap!"

"Yeah," she continued, "I met him and he was really nice. My dad knows someone who knew someone who knew someone who got me an interview."

Trying desperately to play it cool, I asked, "They wouldn't be hiring new interns, would they?"

Melanie encouraged me, "You should totally do it! I'll

give you the number of the woman who hires interns. Just don't tell her you got it from me."

I clutched the contact info Melanie gave me in my pocket for the rest of the day, folding it over and over again as I planned what to say when I finally made the call. It all turned out to be astonishingly easy, though. I just said, "Hello. My name is Ross and I'd like to be an intern."

They must have been hard up for free labor, because I had an interview the very next day.

OMG, right? This was officially my first big Hollywood meeting, so it was imperative that I looked flawlessly put together. But since I only had ten dollars to my name, it was time for me to get creative.

I had two things to do: First, swing by 7-Eleven to grab a Super Big Gulp Diet Coke. Keeping my energy up was essential. Next, I had to take a trip to the local thrift store. Thrift stores are *amazing*! I love the thrill of the hunt, so imagine my delight when I found a charmingly retro olive green suit in my exact size! Sure the sleeves were too short, there was a hole in the crotch and, judging by the smell, it had belonged to a person who must have hoarded cats. But it also boasted something I couldn't resist—a $7 price tag. And if you're doing the math, after the Big Gulp and the suit, I was left with about $1.50—just enough for three hard-shelled tacos at Taco Bell (the normal tacos, not the fancy Supreme ones with a generous squirt of sour cream—I'll never understand why they're double the price for just a dollop of Daisy).

I showed up at NBC for my interview the next day having studied for hours and hours the previous night. No, I didn't research the history of *The Tonight Show* or Jay Leno. Instead, I spent those hours rehearsing how to sit down in my suit while hiding the unfortunate hole in the crotch of my new (well, new to me) discount trousers. My dreams were at stake here, people, and I wasn't about to let a fashion faux pas be my fatal flaw.

I made a mental note to always cross my legs the "lady way" (knee on knee) and not the "macho way" (ankle on knee). To help rehearse for my big *Tonight Show* interview, I enlisted my roommate Ryan to be on crotch patrol—an act of true friendship—diligently watching me sit, cross, uncross, and stand over and over again while keeping his eagle eye squarely between my legs. It occurs to me now that the whole issue could've been solved with a simple sewing kit, but sadly, the gift of *Project Runway* had not yet been given to the world, and I knew no better.

I put a ton of thought and energy into my fancy Hollywood business attire, only to walk in and find that the woman who was interviewing me was a high-powered, no-nonsense entertainment executive wearing sweat pants! Yes, sweat pants! Ugh! I never thought that I'd feel overdressed in my fashionably flammable second-hand suit, but I'd underestimated the power of Casual Friday.

About thirty minutes into the interview, I think the casually elastic-waisted NBC executive could sense my unabashed eagerness to work in the entertainment industry and warned me, "This is a hard job. It's not all about Hollywood and show business glamor. In fact, this job is not about that at all. It's about getting the work done behind the scenes, and that's not always fun or pretty."

I thought for a second. She might have been right, but I wasn't scared. I leaned in closer, lowered my voice and, in almost a whisper, asked her, "Do you know those garbage cans at McDonald's? The ones with the flaps where you dump your tray? Well, when I worked at the Micky D's in Mount Vernon, Washington, I had to crawl inside those cans and scrub off the dried Big Mac secret sauce every day for $4.50 an hour. It wasn't fun or pretty, either. But I would do that here, for free, just to be a part of things. *That's* how badly I want this."

She reached out to shake my hand. "Can you start on Monday?"

When I got home that night, I just couldn't shut up about my great news. I told my friends, "I can't believe it. I'm going to be an intern at the freakin' *Tonight Show*! I know it's totally unpaid and I'm at the very bottom of the showbiz totem pole, but I just feel like it's the start of something big."

It had finally happened. Even though I wasn't technically earning a living, my television career was officially underway. And little did anyone know, it was the beginning of the most outrageous story involving an intern since Monica Lewinsky.

Chapter Five

ROSS THE INTERN 2: HE WORKS HARD FOR NO MONEY

I couldn't sleep the night before my first day as an intern at *The Tonight Show With Jay Leno*. I tossed and turned for hours in my dorm room bunk bed, letting my imagination run wild. Would I get to meet Jay Leno himself? Would I make a whole new group of fancy Hollywood friends? Who will be my secret Santa at the *Tonight Show* Christmas party?

In reality, my first day in show business was decidedly unglamorous and utterly exhausting, just as promised at my interview. My job didn't require merciless manual labor, but the sheer amount of tedious tasks was overwhelming.

Day one of my internship included running around the NBC studio all day making copies, sending faxes, and bringing tapes to *this* person, who needed me to bring something to *that* person, who needed me to fill their printer with ink and then pick up the lunch orders. But, uh-oh! Wait, a minute! The lady in accounting forgot to mention that she doesn't like mustard, so I've got to go get her a new tuna sandwich even though she has perfectly good legs and could totally get her own damn sandwich, but I'm gonna do it because I'm just an intern who isn't getting paid *anything*. But I'd better thank my lucky stars because there are like 5 billion other people who would take my unpaid, thankless job in a heartbeat, so don't screw it up, sweetheart!

I loved it. It was high energy and high pressure, and most important, we were making television, people. After a lifetime of being a viewer, I had crossed over and, even though my contribution was minuscule, I was a part of it nonetheless. I felt both exhilarated and validated.

Without question, the very best moment of my first day was when Jay Leno approached me to introduce himself. I was hurrying down a hallway between errands when I glanced up and saw someone who looked eerily like Jay Leno walking toward me. It took about a millisecond for me to realize that it was, in fact, Jay Leno himself. It's weird, but my first thought was, *Wow. In person, he really does look exactly like Jay Leno.*

I don't know what I expected him to look like, but it was surreal to see someone that famous up close. He was more tan than I expected, and it was odd to see him out of a suit and tie. Instead, he wore the denim-on-denim shirt-and-jeans ensemble that I've come to know as his off-camera uniform. Not many people can pull that off (or should even try, for that matter), but on Jay it looked great.

"Young person," Jay cheerily boomed as he approached. Oh my God, he *sounded* just like Jay Leno, too! "I'm Jay."

I remember thinking it was both ridiculous and very humble that he introduced himself by name, as if anybody in America wouldn't know who he was. He extended his hand

and asked me my name. As we shook hands, I stammered, "I...I'm Ross."

He continued down the hallway smiling. "Welcome to showbiz, kid."

Seriously. It was like a movie. Totally weird, but completely fantastic.

A few weeks into my internship, I had things pretty much figured out. On a typical day, I'd leave my dorm two hours before I had to be at the NBC studio at 8:30 in the morning, slogging through Los Angeles traffic the entire commute. Once I arrived, I'd begin the task of distributing mail to the producers and writers. When that was finished, I'd stock the office kitchen until lunchtime. For an industry that demands that those in front of the camera be fit and trim, it might surprise you to learn that, in every television office, set and trailer, there is food *everywhere.* It's called Craft Services. And for everyone, except people like lowly interns, it's totally free. If you're a higher-up raking in the big bucks, you'll never have to pay for a granola bar or a fist full of Red Vines ever again.

Despite all these free snacks, the bigwigs still needed a proper lunch (yeah, that's free for them, too) and it was my responsibility to make it happen. This was my favorite part of the day, not only because I've always loved lunch in general, but because I had a totally illegal food smuggling operation going on that I've still never told my bosses at NBC about.

Okay, don't judge me. Remember, I was in college, I had no money, and I was working for free way later than my beloved dining hall was open. I was begging my mom for gas money just to be able to drive to my internship in the morning, so I certainly didn't have cash to eat out every day, let alone buy groceries. I was in college-survival mode and had no other choice. So, imagine how agonizing it was for an unpaid intern with an unhealthy relationship with food to not only pick up lunches for the *Tonight Show* writers and producers, but also listen to their downright pornographic orders. "Ross, could you snatch me a hot, juicy burger smothered in gooey jack cheese and loaded with thick cut bacon?"

It was sheer torture! Totally inhumane! You've heard of blue balls? I had blue belly!

So here's what I did, and it sounds like I'm describing a scene straight out of *The Pink Panther*, but I'm absolutely not kidding. When I'd grab the food from the NBC cafeteria, I'd *accidentally* add one extra daily special to the order. Oopsies! Then, on my way back to the offices, I would *accidentally* "misplace" the extra entree behind a huge potted plant. Oopsies again! Once I was on my own lunch break, I'd *accidentally* "find" the "misplaced" lunch behind the plant and *accidentally* devour it without even chewing, like a snake swallows a mouse. Oopsie-doodle-do!

It was probably *technically* against the law and I probably *technically* should've been fired, but you have to admit, it was also *technically* kind of genius.

I was living on the edge! But even with the excitement of my daily cafeteria heist, the day-to-day tasks of office maintenance bored me. At the same time, I knew I was surrounded by some of the top minds in television, and I wasn't about to let the opportunity to pick their brains pass me by.

I'd dreamed of working in TV my entire life, and these people were actually living my dream.

I wanted to learn from these insightful and accomplished professionals, so I asked the receptionist to send out an e-mail asking if any writers or producers would be willing to meet with an eager intern who had a lot of questions. Thankfully, despite their high-pressure jobs and hectic schedules, one of the busy writers actually responded!

His name was Anthony, and he was a relatively new writer on the show. I had seen him around the studio, but didn't know him well, beyond delivering mail to his office. He was in his midthirties, Italian, from New York, and he looked like the handsome lovechild of Adam Sandler and Ralph Macchio.

We made an appointment to meet at his office the next day, and I arrived with, like, a thousand questions. He answered each one politely, getting a kick out of my enthusiasm. Having only interacted with Anthony as an intern, bringing him his lunch and FedEx packages, I couldn't help but feel intimidated as I sat across from him in his office. But it wasn't long before the intern-writer dynamic melted away and we actually began to bond, sharing stories of growing up and our mutual adoration for all things related to Hollywood. I was grateful for his time and made sure not to overstay my welcome.

"Well, thank you so much for this," I said as I got up from my chair and prepared to leave.

"Sure, buddy. Hey, really quick," Anthony asked before I left, "is it worth it, coming here every day and busting your ass for free?"

I answered instantly, without thinking, "One hundred percent, yes. Because I love TV and I'm gonna be a talk show host someday."

He chuckled, assuming I was joking. I wasn't. After quickly realizing I was serious, he added, "All right... Well, I hope you do it, buddy! I can say I knew you when."

My internship lasted only three months, but the lessons I learned and the appreciation I have now for the amount of work that goes into producing a TV show—from makeup to wardrobe, to the prop department to sound—will last a lifetime.

I was reflecting on these lessons as I drove in for my last day of work. At that point, I had a hectic week of finals to prepare for, the holidays were right around the corner and I had already received my letter of recommendation from the *Tonight Show* producers.

Truth time? There was a moment when I considered calling in sick and skipping my last day. I mean, there were a gazillion things I needed to take care of before the end of the semester that, frankly, seemed much more pressing. But I wanted to honor my obligations and finish strong.

About an hour before show time that day, I was refilling the stapler in the copy room when I received a message instructing me to "go see Joe."

There was only one Joe it could be—the *Tonight Show* head writer (and a dead ringer for Ray Romano). An intern called into the head writer's office? This could not be good.

My interactions with Joe up to that point were...well, come to think of it, we had never actually interacted, and he scared the crap out of me. This was the man who, along with

Jay Leno, was responsible for the most-watched monologue on late-night television and helped to create the *Tonight Show*'s most iconic segments, including "Jay Walking" and "Headlines."

In a panic, I racked my brain for a reason behind the call, but the only thing I could come up with was that I had done something terribly wrong. But what? Then I remembered, "Oh my God, the lunches!"

I knew for certain that the jig was up. I had been caught. There was no doubt, I was about to be forced to watch grainy black-and-white surveillance footage of myself scarfing down embezzled beef and stolen salmon. I prepared myself to learn a very valuable lesson: how to be fired in show business.

Have you ever seen the movie *The Green Mile*? It's about a guy on death row, and the Green Mile was what they called his final walk toward the electric chair. That final scene was so over-the-top dramatic and also *exactly* how I felt walking toward Joe's office that day. I could hear the film's theme music in my head, intense and building slowly. First came the strings. I lingered on the stairway, leading up to the second floor. Then the French horns joined in and my stomach began to turn. *Oh no,* I thought. *What will I tell my mom?*

Next, the music continued in my head with a single snare drum, matching the pounding in my chest. My mind continued racing: *Maybe they'll even arrest me. Oh no! My life will never be the same again! What will my prison-bitch name be? Will it be mandatory that I wear one of those hideous orange jumpsuits? I simply can't wear orange—not with my skin tone!*

And, for the record, my prison bitch name would be Muffin Top.

The film score in my head continued with trumpets wailing out of nowhere, like police sirens. *I can't go to the slammer! Who's going to tape* Dawson's Creek *for me?*

An ominous timpani drum began beating, perfectly timed with each step I took toward Joe's door. *BOOM! BOOM! BOOM!*

Here I was, the frenzied climax of the theme music still orchestrating my every move. I had to be strong and accept my fate. Turning the office doorknob with a shaking hand, I heard the climactic crash of cymbals, and suddenly the music in my head went completely silent. I could never have imagined what awaited me on the other side of that door. It wasn't at all what I had expected. But I was right about one thing—my life would never be the same again.

Chapter Six

ROSS THE INTERN 3: FLOATING "ON-AIR"

Deny it if you will, but I know you've all had those fantasy moments in front of the bathroom mirror, accepting your pretend Oscar that's actually a bottle of shampoo. Deep down, we all know that those kind of Hollywood fantasies rarely, if ever, come true. Which is why, when something like that actually *did* happen to me, it felt like a freaky, out-of-body experience. I know it sounds so clichéd, but it really was like watching a play, and the main character was me.

I was sitting across from Joe, the *Tonight Show* head writer. When he first asked me what should have been a simple question, it was as if he was speaking German. It just didn't compute. Confused, I asked, "I'm sorry, can you repeat that?"

He leaned back in his seat, folded his arms across his chest and repeated the question so casually, he might as well have been offering me a breath mint. "What would you think about coming out on stage during tonight's taping, meeting George Clooney, and leaving with him to be our correspondent at the red carpet premiere of *Ocean's Eleven*?"

This time I heard him loud and clear. "Yes, I would very much like to do that."

You'd think I would've totally lost my shit, but instead I remained calm and had a moment of absolute clarity. The thought simply occurred to me: *Oh, this is how it's all going to happen. This will be my story. Remember this for the book you'll write one day.*

I later learned that a professional comic was originally scheduled to cover the premiere but had dropped out at the last minute. In what I consider a stroke of pure genius (if I do say so myself), another writer named Larry Jacobson half-jokingly suggested that they send "the intern with that voice" instead. I don't know if Larry will ever really know the impact his offhand suggestion has had on my life. If you're reading this, Larry: thank you, like a lot.

Of course, I had a ton of questions. "What should I wear?"

"What you're wearing is fine."

"What do you want me to ask the celebs?"

"Don't prepare anything, just ask the first thing that pops into your head."

I could certainly do that. "Will this really be on TV?"

"Maybe. We don't know for sure. First, we have to see if what you tape is good or not."

Um, no pressure.

I was told that I had one hour before heading out to the premiere, which was just enough time to call my mom and deliver the big news. I figured I'd play it cool at first, you know, for dramatic effect. I sounded totally blasé when she picked up. "Hey Mom. How are you? What are you doing?"

"Hi, sweetie! Oh God, well, I had a hell of a day. First, your dad wanted me to make tacos for dinner tonight, but Thrifty Foods was out of the lean ground beef that I like, so I think we're just gonna go to the Mexico Café instead."

Okay, enough taco talk. I interrupted her and broke my big news. I could almost hear her heart beating through the phone. "Oh, dear God. Just a sec, honey. I'll call you right back."

My mom's going to kill me for this, but I made a promise to you, dear reader, to be honest and this is just too good not to share. My mother's reaction to any big news, be it good or bad, is always *instant* diarrhea. I wouldn't lie to you, because if I did, I would have just wasted thirty seconds looking up how to spell *diarrhea*.

Minutes later, after doing her business, she called back. *"Oh my God. Oh my God! Honey!* This is *huge.* If you do half as well at this as you did when you starred in *The Hobbit* in the seventh grade, you're going to knock it out of the park, I just know it!"

God bless my mom. I *was* really good in *The Hobbit*.

I spent the next forty-five minutes just thinking by myself as the enormity of the situation began to sink in. I knew I was getting the chance I had always hoped for, but I was also aware that I was exposing myself to possible rejection and ridicule on a national level. I mean, I got it. I knew who I was. That childhood moment with the bully in the spinach field wasn't an isolated incident. As a proud, high-pitched, grown-up oddity, I had faced homophobia on a daily basis, and for a split second, I questioned whether or not this was a risk I was prepared to take. *The Tonight Show* may have been willing to celebrate my eccentricities and give me a chance, but would the show's middle-American audience do the same?

I knew initially, the viewers were probably going to laugh *at* me. Why wouldn't they? Who was this over-the-top cartoon on their TVs? But I also knew that a person couldn't sustain a career by constantly being the butt of the joke. I had so much more to offer than that, and I felt I really had the skills needed to be a bone fide broadcaster. So, if I wanted this to work, I had to find a way to get the audience to laugh *with* me, not *at* me. That is, if I wanted this to be more than just a onetime thing.

What happened next was surreal. Suddenly the very same people whose coffee I had just delivered earlier in the day were prepping me to go on air to meet the sexiest man alive, George Clooney (and that's not just my opinion—*People* magazine made it official in both 1997 *and* 2006, thank you very much).

Minutes before the big moment, I was standing backstage in the blue zip-up fleece jacket I had found just days before on the clearance rack at JCPenney, taking in my surroundings. I stared at the doorway where every celebrity I could imagine had walked through to greet Jay Leno on the *Tonight Show* stage and couldn't believe I was just about to walk through it myself. I heard the audience laughing as Jay and George chatted mere feet away from me. I closed my eyes and took a deep breath, trying to shake off my nerves and focus, when I suddenly heard Jay Leno saying my name.

"We have this young intern, Ross Mathews, who just loves all things Hollywood."

Okay, this is bonkers. Jay Leno just said my name on TV. There was no turning back now.

He continued, "Would you mind, George, if he went with you to your premiere tonight and interviewed the other stars of the film?"

This couldn't possibly get any more bizarre. Jay Leno and George Clooney were having a conversation about me. Whoa.

George replied, "Sure."

"All right," Jay continued, "Come on out here, Ross."

Roberta, the stage manager, shoved me through the doors and onto the *Tonight Show* stage for the very first time. I was so captivated by the lights and cameras and audience, I barely even noticed George (and you *know* your head is spinning when you don't notice George Clooney right in front of you).

I said quietly, almost to myself, "Wow, so this is what it looks like from here."

Those were my first words on national television.

In a Hollywood minute, I was in an NBC van headed to the famous Village Theater with a production crew consisting of Kevin the cameraman, Kenny the audio engineer, Scott the talent coordinator, Izzy the production assistant, and Anthony the writer (yes, the same Anthony whose brain I had picked just weeks earlier). These people were basically strangers to me then, but they have continued to work with me on all my *Tonight Show* segments and I now consider them family. But back then I was just a kid in a van with a bunch of scary grown-ups.

I attempted small talk. "So, this should be a lot of fun, right?"

Anthony looked up from his notes and tried to calm my nerves. "Relax, Ross, and have a good time. We just thought it might be funny to see what happened if we sent someone from the office out to talk with celebs. Just be you and it'll be fine."

"Oh, I get it. Like 'Ross the Intern meets the stars' kinda thing?"

"'Ross the Intern'..." Anthony repeated. "I like that."

The *Ocean's Eleven* premiere was about as star-studded as you can get, and the scene at the red carpet was insane. Westwood Boulevard was closed down for the event and, by the time we got there, hundreds of fans were lining the sidewalks behind barricades, media outlets from all over the world were crowding the press line, and security was being a real pain in the butt. It was such a tornado of chaos that even though our entire crew had the proper credentials, we were all denied access to the red carpet.

"What the hell?" I asked Anthony. "We can't even get in!"

Laughing, he yelled to Kevin the cameraman, "Start rolling now!"

Then he turned toward me and gave me some directions. "Okay, Ross, just talk to the camera and describe what's going on."

I looked into the camera lens, took a quick breath, and just pretended like I was talking to my mom. "It's nuts! There's security here and they're not letting me in, but George Clooney is right over there and I promise I'll get to him no matter what."

"Good!" Anthony yelled.

When security finally granted us access to the press line, we muscled our way into position. I stepped to the edge of the red carpet, took a quick glance at my microphone with the *Tonight Show* logo, and looked back up to see someone familiar standing in front of me. It was David Duchovny from *The X-Files* waiting for me to ask him a question.

I don't even remember what we talked about, but I do remember turning to the camera with a devilish smile as he walked away and saying, "David Duchovny was my first."

I could hear Anthony and the crew gasp and burst into laughter. I knew I was on to something and made the decision to just trust myself to say the first thing that came into my mind.

From there, the interviews got even better. I shed all inhibition and fell into a natural rhythm and creative zone, losing track of time while chitchatting with one huge celeb after another. When I saw George Clooney making his way down the press line, I yelled out his name, purposely pronouncing it the Spanish way ("Jorge, Jorge my man!"). I shared an awkward moment with Matt Damon while having him hold up a picture of Carolina, a fellow *Tonight Show* intern who had a crush on him. I got into a minifight with Casey Affleck when he called me a toad (we buried the hatchet a few minutes later), and left Brad Pitt virtually speechless by shamelessly flirting with him.

It felt amazing, like I was in some kind of autopilot mode. It was like something was in control of me, and I said and did things I would have never normally said or done. I mean, when I see a famous person in my everyday life, I don't run up to them and make a scene. But when I was on that red carpet that night, nothing was off-limits and my only goal was to create a funny and memorable moment with them. To this day, that's what always happens when I'm on the job and have a microphone in my hand. I'm still me, but I'm an amped-up, heightened version of myself. Think Beyonce as her alter-ego Sasha Fierce, if you know what I mean.

When the red carpet finally wrapped up, I let out a huge sigh of relief. Pushing up the sleeves of my fleece jacket, I turned to the crew and asked, "How was that?"

Anthony was the first to speak. "Where in the hell did all that come from?"

"Was it okay? Did I talk too much? I know, I can be annoying."

"No, not annoying. I feel like I just saw a career being made."

I know what you're thinking. This sounds too cheesy to be true, like the end of *Rudy*. But I'm not kidding, this is how it really happened. I'm not trying to toot my own tooter. Anthony really did say that, and the crew really did hug me afterward and told me they were thrilled to have witnessed that moment.

After seeing the footage the next day, the producers immediately asked me to cover the upcoming *Vanilla Sky* premiere. Next, they sent me to Salt Lake City for a month to cover the Winter Olympics, and then to the Academy Awards, and so on. Now, somehow, it's over eleven years later and I'm the longest-running correspondent in *Tonight Show* history.

Some people call what happened to me a lucky break. Kind of, but I don't really believe in luck. I believe in

Oprah, which is why I quote her all the time. I once heard her say (and I'm sort of paraphrasing, here), "There's no such thing as luck. Luck is when opportunity meets preparation."

I was prepared for my opportunity, and I made the most of it. I think that's why my dream of being on TV has, and continues to, come true. Whatever your dream may be, make sure you're prepared, because you never know when your own George Clooney might come a'knockin'.

Chapter Seven

A THIESSEN TO CELEBRATE

The year was 1995. Her name was Tiffani-Amber Thiessen. A star so nice, they named her thrice. And, no matter what else she accomplishes in life, to me, she will always hold the title of the First Celebrity I Ever Met.

I loved her the moment I saw her on *Saved by the Bell* as the irrepressible Kelly Kapowski, the cheerleader with a heart as big as her bangs. She was the epitome of cutting-edge nineties fashion with her skintight bike shorts, acid-wash denim, and Day-Glo scrunchies. But what I think I loved even more than her totally tubular wardrobe was the fact that while she was obviously the most popular girl at Bayside High, she never let it go to her beautiful head.

You'd think I would have considered her a threat, since we both had eyes for the blond hair and white teeth known as Zack Morris, played with verve and aplomb by Mark-Paul Gosselaar, another actor blessed with not just talent but three names.

Yep, she had the hair, the clothes, *and* the man. In short, she had every right to be a stuck-up snob, but she some-how managed to remain surprisingly sweet. Now *that's* my kind of gal.

When I heard on my local AM radio station that she was going to be making an appearance at the Bon Marché department store in downtown Seattle, only sixty miles—a mere hop, skip, and a jump—from my sleepy Norman Rock-wellian hometown, you can bet your bottom dollar I was going to be there. I wouldn't miss it for the world. It was a no-freakin'-brainer!

I was only fifteen and couldn't drive, so I convinced one of my best girlfriends to join me. Molly was one year my senior and the proud owner of not only a driver's li-cense and the new Rachel haircut, but a gleaming white Geo Prizm—complete with one of those fancy new CD players—that her parents gave her when she turned six-teen (jealous!).

We sang TLC's "Waterfalls" at the top of our lungs all the way down to Seattle. Once there, we waited in line for—no joke—three hours, spending every second planning exactly what I should say to Tiffani-Amber Thiessen when I finally reached the front of the line.

"It's important for me," I told Molly, slowly drawing out each word to fully illustrate just how much thought I'd put into all of this, "that I let Ms. Thiessen know"—pensive pause, hand on heart—"*how* her work has touched me. I don't want her to just"—dramatic sigh—"*get* that I care, I want her to get"—looking up as if searching the heavens for just the right word—"*why* she made me care." Tilt head to one side. "You know what I mean?" Close eyes, smile, and nod.

Eventually, as we slowly edged closer to the autograph table, I stopped talking to Molly altogether. I didn't want to be rude, but this was no time for idle chitchat. I needed to go inward, disappear into myself in order to fully prepare what I was going to say during my big moment with Tiffani-Amber Thiessen. I rehearsed my speech over and over again in my head until it was simply perfect. I had it down—every word, every nuance, every subtlety. It was, quite frankly, nothing short of a masterpiece. I knew deep down in my heart that even if Tiffani-Amber Thiessen met a thousand people that day, she'd remember me the very best. Perhaps she'd even tell me so, under her breath, of course, in an effort to not offend the less-memorable, so-called biggest fans in line behind me.

I mean, she might be so moved by my heartfelt words and obvious dedication that she'd even ask for my home phone number, which I'd gladly give her, nonchalantly mentioning that my parents pay extra for three-way calling so we could also totally call Zack Morris and just shoot the shit if she ever wanted to, but no biggie.

Sure, she was a big Hollywood star and I was just a fifteen-year-old with stars in my eyes and zits on my chin, but I knew the moment we met the planets would align and we would be inseparable, just like the Siamese twins I'd seen on a recent episode of *Rikki Lake.*

The three hours spent in line—180 minutes, 10,800 seconds—seemed to go by in an instant, and suddenly I was being rudely yanked from my daydream by a large security guard who barked, "Hey, kid! You in the green jacket! You're up."

Huh?!? Wait a minute. I was already at the front of the line?!? But I wasn't ready!

Oh my God, I thought. *How's my hair? How's my breath? Why are my palms sweating? I'm next? It couldn't possibly be my turn already! What was that brilliant-but-genuine thing I planned on saying to her? I forget. I forget!!! I FORGET WHAT I WAS GONNA—*

"What's your name, sweetie?"

I blinked and suddenly there she was, Tiffani-Amber Thiessen, all three names of her. Not in class next to A. C. Slater or in Mr. Belding's office or slinging burgers at The Max—she was in front of me and she was asking my name. Holy crapballs.

The weirdest thing about getting up close and personal with famous people is seeing their imperfections. Now, Tiffani-Amber, if I may be so bold as to go Thiessen-less, is a lovely lady and she looked every inch the TV star that day with her impossibly shiny hair and Malibu Barbie tan. But, when I got *really* close, I saw something that threw me for a major loop: A teeny tiny, itty-bitty glob of mascara in the corner of her left eye.

No biggie, right? It happens to everyone. Stars, they're just like us? Go figure! Perhaps celebrities weren't quite as perfect as I'd thought. Now, if I found myself in this situation today, it wouldn't be a big deal at all. I would probably just whisper, "Hey girl, you gotta little gunk in your eye."

But the fifteen year-old me didn't know how to handle it. In fact, I had become instantly obsessed with this unexpected eye booger. It was like a big black punctuation mark, the period that was bringing time to a screeching halt.

As silly as it sounds, I couldn't fathom the idea of my perfect K-Pow—the very first celebrity I had ever come face to face with—having an imperfection. And although this blemish was clearly temporary and merely surface level, it was still the ultimate distraction. I couldn't let it go. I mean, how could this go unnoticed? Didn't she have people on the payroll looking out for such disasters? If they weren't going to tell her, then maybe I should! Or better yet, I could simply take control and make things right, make her perfect again. I was imagining myself gently swabbing Tiff's eye with a Q-tip like her chubby knight in shining armor, when I heard what sounded like a record skipping. "What's your name?... Your name...?...Name...?"

I could hear Tiffani-Amber asking the question, and for the love of God I wanted to respond, but I couldn't think of the answer. I heard Molly's voice just behind me, answering on my behalf. "Ross. His name is Ross."

Tiffani-Amber asked, "Ross, would you like an autograph?"

Again, I said nothing. My mind was blank. Molly, still acting as my interpreter, piped up. "Yes, he'd love one."

Tiffani-Amber pulled a head shot from the stack beside her, signed it and pushed it across the table. "Ross, honey," she asked, "Do you want to take a picture together?"

Molly shoved me forward and chimed, "Yes!"

Tiffani leaned in close. We were literally just inches apart now. I was being pulled into the orbit of a real star and she smelled like a mixture of honeysuckle and the Hollywood sign. *Divine.* When the camera clicked, I felt a flash of light burn my eyes, and when my sight returned a few moments later, I somehow found myself back on the Seattle streets with Molly.

"Did it really happen?" I asked Molly while rubbing my eyes. "Or was it all just a dream?!?"

Molly gleefully recounted the horror story of my doomed Thiessen interaction. "My favorite part," Molly squealed, "was when you forgot your own name!"

She was lying. That couldn't have happened. "You're lying, Molly. That couldn't have happened."

She was in hysterics now, nearly hyperventilating with laughter. "And then I had to practically prop you up for a picture!"

"*You shut your stupid mouth, stupid!!!*"

I went too far. I'd never lashed out like that before. Molly realized that for me to say something that harsh, she had really crossed a line. Regaining her composure, she wrapped a comforting arm around my shoulders. "Okay, okay, I'm sorry. It wasn't really *that* bad. I mean, it was kinda cute in a way. You were like a clueless puppy or an adorable little toddler who just woke up, all dazed and confused and stuff? You know?"

I appreciated her attempt at kindness, but she wasn't helping. This was the absolute worst thing that had ever happened in the history of the world. I couldn't help but think my life was basically over. I mean, how could it have all gone so terribly wrong?

Tiffani probably thinks I'm a grade-A idiot, I thought to myself. *Maybe she's even thinking about it at this very moment, laughing at my meet-and-greet meltdown. She's probably telling her hair and makeup people the story right now. I bet her bitchy hairstylist thinks it's the funniest thing he's ever heard. "Oh girl," he's cackling while smoothing her flyaways, "you've gotta tell Mark-Paul about this loser!"*

I don't handle tragedy well. I never have. And I dealt with it that day the way I always do: by loading up on carbs. I zeroed in on a street vendor, dug a whopping $2.50 out of my pocket, and splurged on a big soft pretzel. I ripped into that salty knot of baked dough like a pit bull. I took my frustration out on that defenseless twisted treat, pathetically chewing the pain away. I stood there with bright yellow mustard smeared across my lips, my cheeks bulging like an insane, nut-hoarding squirrel. That's when Molly perkily chirped, "Well, at least it couldn't get any worse."

But then it did.

As we rounded a corner, I nearly walked right into—you guessed it—The Thiessen, who was exiting the shopping center with her entourage. We were once again face-to-face—mine stained with mustard and hers looking as flawless as ever (someone must have pointed out the eye booger because it was now gone).

I'm not sure why or how it happened, dear reader, but my circuits became overloaded, my wires crossed and, for some reason, my mouth started spewing both words *and* chunks of chewed pretzel at her. I was standing less than two feet away, yelling, "TIFFANI-AMBER THIESSEN! IT'S ME, ROSS! REMEMBER? I JUST MET YOU A LITTLE WHILE AGO! ROSS?!? REMEMBER ME?!?"

What happened next reminds me of footage of the attempted assassination of Ronald Reagan (YouTube it). Tiffani-Amber's handlers immediately kicked into Code

Red, forcefully ushering her away from the high-pitched nutcase (yours truly) and into a car that then sped away, leaving only myself and a dumbstruck Molly. She stared at me with her mouth agape and an expression of shock, disbelief, and pity on her face.

After what seemed like an unbearably long and awkward silence, Molly once again put a reassuring arm around my shoulder, took a deep breath, and quietly said, "Well, you were right."

I looked at her like a sad little cartoon character with question marks in my eyes. "Of all the people she met today," Molly continued, "Tiffani-Amber Thiessen will totally remember you the very best."

Chapter Eight

YOU BETTER WORK (AND A LIFELONG SECRET REVEALED)

I entered the work force when I was thirteen years old. I was inspired by my brother Eric who, after only six months of employment at the Royal Fork Buffet, had worked his way up from lowly dishwasher to assistant to the assistant head cook—a meteoric rise I had only witnessed, up until that point, in the Melanie Griffith–Harrison Ford classic, *Working Girl.*

The Royal Fork (which my dad lovingly referred to as "the Royal Fuck") afforded my brother a lavish lifestyle of which I couldn't have been more jealous. His new paycheck was elevating everything about him. Suddenly he had gorgeous orange highlights in his hair, he started wearing No Fear T-shirts like those fancy kids who lived in two-story houses, he smelled better (Drakkar Noir will *always* be his signature scent) and, most important, he no longer had to choke down store-brand cheese doodle snacks from the day-old bin at the grocery store like everyone else in our family. No ma'am, he indulged his maturing palate with real-deal, highfalutin name-brand Cheetos along with his school lunches. He was becoming so sophisticated, in fact, that he opted for the delicate puffed variety as opposed to the simple crunchy version the rest of us Mathews—and other "salt of the earth" types—shamelessly scarfed down on a regular basis.

A-hole. It wasn't fair. I wanted a better life (and better snacks), too. And thus began my impressively varied string of childhood jobs. Seriously, as a kid, I had just about every job you can imagine short of making knockoff Gucci wallets in a run-down factory.

After dabbling briefly in the cutthroat spinach business in a nearby field (as discussed ad nauseam in chapter 1), I then signed on to spend my summer vacation working the conveyor belt at a local tulip and daffodil farm, separating the flower bulbs from dirt clods for eight hours a day. I was literally doing the dirty work.

There wasn't a ton of socializing going on, mostly because we were all rendered temporarily deaf due to the loud roar of the equipment, but also because 90 percent of my fellow coworkers didn't speak English. (Education tip from Uncle Ross: take Spanish or Japanese—a language you can actually *use*—maybe even French, if you plan on being a chef or a sexy maid. I took Latin, which, with apologies to my high school Latin teacher, turned out to be as useless as a thesaurus on the set of *Jersey Shore*.)

I spent most of my workday nodding my head in agreement to whatever my coworkers were saying (those exotic rolled Rs can be surprisingly persuasive) and pretending I was anywhere other than where I was. This sure as hell was no Royal Fork Buffet. This was a royal forking pain in my ass.

That's the thing about truly shitty jobs—they teach you precisely what you never, *ever* want to do again. Sorting filthy flower bulbs proved to be mind-numbingly boring manual labor that left my hands super-rough and über-dry if I didn't wear the company-issued, industry-standard yellow rubber gloves (*so* not my color!). This was a no-win situation, however, because my hands got all pruney and sweaty and gross if I wore the gloves for too long. So I kept alternating every fifteen minutes or so: gloves on, gloves off, gloves on, gloves off. That maddening on/off routine was torture to maintain, and occasionally I would be distracted by my actual job duties, making the tragic mistake of accidentally leaving the gloves on for too long. This resulted in both my wrinkled hands and my soggy gloves smelling exactly like boiled hot dogs. No joke: *exactly*.

It was revolting, but for some reason I couldn't stop smelling them. Despite my utter revulsion and against my better judgment, I would hold my hands and gloves up to my face and huff them. I was like a wholesome sitcom version of those poor dazed souls on *Intervention* who compulsively inhale magic marker, spray paint, or gasoline fumes.

Puh-lease, keep your judgment to yourself. I know I'm not the only person who sometimes finds sick pleasure in horrible smells. Don't for one minute pretend you haven't delighted in the disgust of a dirty sock, long-expired dairy product, or your own funky BO. Don't you dare turn your nose up at my courageous admission when you know your nose has done the exact same thing.

It quickly became obvious to everyone at the plant that bulb farming just wasn't for me. Eventually my supervisor,

Marta, staged an intervention of her own. She gently pulled me away from the conveyor belt, looked deep into my eyes while shaking her head and said, "Ross, honey, we all like you here, but you're spending too much time smelling your gloves. This is your third warning and I'm afraid we're going to have to let you go."

Fair enough. She had a point. Thank God she said something. Sometimes you need a push. To this day, I can't smell a hot dog without thinking of dear Marta.

After that, I became much more picky when it came to my professional life. I wanted to identify exactly what I was looking for in a job. I knew for certain that I no longer wanted to work outdoors, so a temperature-controlled environment was a *must*. I also wished for a job that connected me with the people. You know, like really up close and personal? Finally, it was imperative that I work in an industry that really ignited a passion within me. The answer was clear: I needed a McJob.

The McDonald's in my hometown got a makeover in about 1992, so it was pretty freakin' cool. The interior color scheme was ultra modern—gray, black, and yellow. They had removed what used to be the kiddie section called Old McDonald's Barn (where, by the way, I celebrated my seventh birthday) and replaced it with an entire wall of TV screens that played McDonald's-sponsored cartoons and music videos on a continuous loop all day long. Awesome.

This was exactly the kind of place that could take my career to the next level. I remember being incredibly nervous when I brought in my application, completed with the lucky pen I was awarded for perfect attendance at my eighth-grade graduation.

Before I handed in my paperwork, I bought a supersized Number One (Big Mac, fries, and a drink), settled into a corner booth, and ate slowly while scoping out the joint. Field research is essential, so I began taking copious notes on a napkin:

> The Blue Shirts tell the Pink Shirts what to do.
> The Blue Shirts must be managers.
> Most of the Blue Shirts have mustaches.
> The boys wear hats.
> The girls wear visors.
> I prefer a visor.
> The guy in the short-sleeved button-up shirt must be in charge.
> He has big arms.
> He must work out.
> He has a mustache, too.
> Note to self: Maybe try to grow a mustache?

As I savored my last remaining french fry, I felt ready. This was the right place for me. After I topped off my Diet Coke (hello, free refills), I marched up to the head guy with the big arms in the too-small shirt and attempted my most professionally cheery greeting. "Excuse me, sir? First off, I *love* your mustache. Second, I was wondering if you were hiring."

Without looking up from the fry machine he snapped, "Fill out an application and bring it back."

"One step ahead of you," I snapped back while whipping out my application with a dramatic flourish and setting it down on the counter.

I don't know if it was my excellent penmanship or the mustache comment, but he hired me immediately. I was in! I was now a proud member of the McDonald's family! Sure, I was thrilled to simply have a job indoors, but it got even better—the perks were beyond my wildest fantasies!

Mr. Mustache told me that I would be starting at *five* dollars an hour (a full fifty cents more than I was making at the ol' bulb farm) and—get this—I was allowed two free items every break, not counting sodas. Because child labor laws were so strict in Washington State (holla!), I got two fifteen-minute breaks and a thirty-minute lunch for every shift I worked. Do the math, people. That translated into how many delicious McDonald's menu items per day? Six. Yep, six whole items. Are you kidding me? I was in hamburger heaven!

Free food is an incredible motivator. I never once dreaded heading in to work because I knew an entire kitchen full of possibilities awaited me, and just about every single one of them could be dipped in BBQ sauce. It was all so fantastically simple. When my break came, I just asked the guy behind the grill for whatever I wanted and he gave it to me like a magic, wish-granting genie.

"I think I'll start with a...yes. Bacon, egg, and cheese biscuit, please. But can you add just a whisper of extra cheese? Thanks. So, that's *one* item. I think I'll wash that down with...Yes, a hash brown. *No!* An apple pie—fruit is healthier."

Breakfast? Check.

Then I worked for about one and a half hours, spending the whole time daydreaming about my next meal.

"Nuggets please. Six of 'em. Throw in a few BBQs and a couple Sweet and Sours. I'm feelin' saucy. Get it? And, umm...are those fries fresh? They are? Okay, then give me a small, no, supersized fry. Thanks!"

Lunch? Check.

Keep in mind, also, that sodas didn't count as one of my allotted items, so by lunch I had consumed enough Diet Coke to fill a kiddie pool.

I was usually rotated to the drive-through position by the latter part of my shift, giving me not only a beautiful view of the parking lot (shared with Shakey's Pizza—yum! Mojo Potatoes, anyone?), but also some privacy to focus on my next break.

"God, I thought my break would never come. Um, let me see.... You know what sounds positively delish? A Filet-O-Fish. But I don't want any cheese on it, please. Just extra tartar sauce. And maybe I'll try one of those hot fudge sundaes for dessert? Hold the nuts, they're kinda fattening, you know? If you spilled a little caramel sauce on it too, I wouldn't be mad at you. Thanks!"

Dinner? Check.

Have you seen the blockbuster documentary *Super Size Me*? Well, I was basically living the plotline. The only good to come out of all the McDonald's food I was consuming on a daily basis was that every couple of months I had to get a brand-spanking-new uniform. The old one must've shrunk or something. Just kidding—I was getting fatter. It was no wonder, considering I was eating enough deep-fried food to feed everyone at a Midwestern county fair. Eventually one of my favorite coworkers, Veronica—a sassy, tell-it-like-it-is Chola mom of cinco—told me one day, "You face is good. But why you so fat for?"

Yes, I was gaining weight, but I was also gaining a much larger friend base. Quick tip? If you work at McDonald's and the most popular girl in school comes in to order, you are the most powerful person in the world. "No, Courtney, this is on me. I insist. It's, like, no biggie. I'll just mark down that you had a coupon. See you at school tomorrow? Maybe we can sit next to each other at lunch?"

Also, I was now getting invited more than ever to hang out and watch TV with friends. I would arrive at their houses right after work, just in time for *Real World: Miami*. Still in my uniform and reeking of saturated fats, I would bring the ultimate hostess gift: two huge bags of whatever was left over when we had closed the restaurant. It's true, the way to someone's heart is indeed through their stomach. And my heaping bags of greasy cheesy treats congealed right around their li'l hearts. I was a *hit*! The BMOC: Big Mac On Campus!

All in all, I was a good employee. I was reliable and courteous, and my McRib-making skills were second to none. I did, though, have an issue with one detail in particular: the uniform rules required that I had to wear a baseball cap instead of a visor. Apparently visors were for the girls only? Umm…this just wasn't right. It was a major *Norma Rae*-style workplace injustice. These were the nineties, for God's sake—'N Sync's Chris Kirkpatrick was a poster boy for the male visor, breaking gender barriers for all of us. It was a brave new world, but my jerky manager, Dwayne (not to be confused with big-armed Mr. Mustache), just didn't get it.

At the time, I had a head full of short, glorious curls (a la early Justin Timberlake, another groundbreaking 'N Sync influence) made perfect by L.A. Looks Firm Hold Gel. There's no way that a ball cap was going to suppress my spirit, or the volume of my hair. Out of the freaking question.

Finally, after much nagging and going above Dwayne's head (can you say "regional manager"?), Dwayne caved in, and I wore my visor proudly alongside the unflinchingly honest Veronica.

"Why you wear girl hat for?"

"Because, Veronica, this is America and, male or female, hat hair doesn't discriminate."

Revolutionary change may sometimes take a while to get used to, but it's possible. You may call me a trailblazer. Okay, I'm fine with that. And I carry that title proudly. If you ever happen to see a male McDonald's employee wearing a visor, tell him I said, "Hello...And you're welcome."

It was a great time for me, and my superiors took notice of my moxie. I was thrilled when I was promoted and transferred to the McDonald's Express in the nearby Cascade Mall, thinking I was being rewarded for my hard work. But little did I know that my quick climb up the fast-food ladder would lead to the downward spiral of my McCareer.

Although I appreciated the convenience of working in the mall, being both retail adjacent and surrounded by countless cuisines (my counter was positioned between a Footlocker and a Sbarro's), it quickly became obvious that, in the eyes of others who worked in the mall, I was food court scum. I was a lowlife. At my old McDonald's, I was a king—the guy who went face to face with stubborn ol'

Dwayne over VisorGate and lived to tell about it. But in the mall world, I was at the bottom of the food chain.

They never said it out loud, but I knew. When Brett from Brookstone ordered an All-American Cheeseburger Meal on his lunch break, his voice dripped with disdain. When Suzanne from Sears picked up her daily medium Dr. Pepper, no ice, she barely even acknowledged me. Screw you, Suzie. I knew you in kindergarten. You couldn't finger-paint then and you can't throw attitude now.

But I couldn't really blame them. Deep down, I knew it was me who was the problem. As much as I loved my McDonald's job, it was beginning to pale in comparison to the other jobs in the mall that, let's face it, were much cooler, cleaner, and just plain less-greasy. Those who worked at the other shops—the "retail people"—seemed so happy. Of course they were happy—they smelled like samples of perfume, not pickles. They wore designer-logo-emblazoned cotton, not condiment-stained polyester. Hell, they drove Hondas! Man, they were living the life, and I wanted in on it.

The time had finally come for me to move on from McDonald's, and I had my sights set on retail. The options in the mall were endless, so I decided to take a leap of faith by quitting my fast-food job altogether, certain I would soon land in greener pastures. I would have been thrilled to work at any of the retail shops: Bar-D-Western (a cowboy-themed clothing store owned by the parents of the Asian girl in my geometry class), the always refreshing Bath and Body Works, or the kiosk in the center of the mall that sold crystal figurines. You haven't lived until you've seen two dozen crystal unicorns glittering in a mirrored display case beneath special halogen track lighting. And just imagine what kind of employee discount I would get on one of those mythical creatures. Fifty, 60 percent off? Oh God!

The problem? Even though I printed my application on mint green paper and spritzed it lightly with my brother's Drakkar Noir, not one store would hire me. Not a single one, not even with my inside connection to my Asian classmate's family. I felt totally betrayed. I mean, she and I had been study buddies!

I almost gave up following what I thought was a particularly successful interview at Afterthoughts (a small boutique that sold bargain, last-minute accessories to complete an outfit—things like headbands, scrunchies, and bangles). I thought I had hit it out of the park at the interview. The manager was in her forties and had hair that went down to her knees. We had a lengthy conversation about how difficult it was to braid that much hair. She showed me her favorite brush. There was definite chemistry, and we had a connection, damn it! But, alas, I never heard back from her. It's so sad, really. I mean, just imagine what I could have done with all that hair. Updos galore.

I was beginning to panic. Like a total idiot, I had already quit McDonald's before I'd locked in a new job. Time was ticking by without cash flowing in. There was a certain lifestyle I had grown accustomed to, and it involved going to the Cineplex on a regular basis—hello, those Meg Ryan movies weren't gonna watch themselves! And do you know how much the cinema charged for Whoppers and an extra large popcorn at the snack bar?!? Unreal! I needed a paycheck and I needed it fast. So there's a lesson here, kids. If you have a steady job that you hate, don't be impulsive and drop it like a hot apple pie right outta the deep fryer. Instead, play it cool, heed the advice of Wilson Phillips, and "Hold on for one more day..."

I found myself jobless, once again a civilian who had to pay for my Diet Coke. Tears filled my eyes after another endless, hungry day of handing out applications when I walked by a store that for some reason, I had never noticed before. I asked my mom about it when I got home.

"What's Lane Bryant?"

"The plus-size store at the mall? Why do you ask?"

"Oh, no reason," I replied, trying to hide my glee. A plus-sized clothing store for women? Was there a more perfect place in the entire world for me to work?!? I'd had a lifelong love affair with full-figured ladies. Delta Burke, Roseanne, Rosie, Oprah—these were my people! If anyone could see my retail potential and take a risk on me, it was gonna be a BBW (Big Beautiful Woman).

I was a tad nervous to apply, fearing that rejection from a big-boned gal would crush my spirit. But the dream of spending eight hours a day assisting large but fashionable gals accentuate their sexy curves and smartly camouflage "trouble areas" lit a fire under my equally plus-sized ass.

"I'm here to apply for a position," I told the lady at the sales counter. She had really cool hair. It was a deep maroon hue with a platinum blonde streak serving as the surprising centerpiece of her bangs. This fantastic creation was longer in the front and kinda spiky in the back. *Very* ahead of its time. Sort of a Kate Gosselin backward mullet. The kind of hairdo that said, *Yeah, I work at the mall, but I have a gay cousin who does hair in the city.*

She smiled. "Really? Well, come on back with me."

Her name was Kend'rah and I liked her a lot. I never got the nerve to ask if she added the apostrophe herself, but I assumed she did. She deserved it. She was just about the coolest person I'd ever met. I yearned to be like her. I even considered, right then and there, changing my name to R'oss.

"Have you ever worked retail before?" she asked while playing with the coiled telephone-cord-like keychain around her wrist, a telltale sign of a retail manager.

I answered honestly. "No, but I shop a lot."

She laughed. I laughed, too. This was the best interview I'd ever had. We chatted for over an hour and, by the time I left, I was officially the only male employee at the Lane Bryant in the Cascade Mall.

Just as I had imagined, working in retail was so much better than working in fast food. Case in point? When there were no customers at McDonald's, I had to stay busy by scrubbing the thick layer of grease behind the deep fryer. "If there's time to lean, there's time to clean!"

But when there were no customers at Lane Bryant, I got to stay "busy" by gossiping with my coworkers and boss Kend'rah about the most recent episode of *Melrose Place* while we folded extra large pairs of stirrup pants. Sure, I didn't get free nuggets at my new job, but I did get to rattle off priceless nuggets to customers like, "Honey, did you leave fifty pounds in the dressing room? Because you look *amazing*!!!"

I was in my element, and I quickly became the number one salesperson in the entire store. No joke. Look it up. I'm sure it's in their records somewhere. I was the best—the Wizard of Waistbands, the Sultan of Stretch Jeans, the Baron of Belts.

It was, by far, the best job I'd ever had. I loved every minute of it, all one and a half years that I worked there. I'd love to say that I'd return to my old position at the company one day, maybe live out my retirement as an assistant manager at the Palm Springs branch. But, dear reader, that will never happen. Ever. Why? Because it's forbidden. Why? Because, dear reader, of what I'm about to tell you—a story I've only shared with one other person, my very best friend who I confessed to only moments after it happened. I haven't even told my mother. She will read it for the first time with all of you. Mom, please sit down. The time has come for me to cleanse myself and undo these shackles of shame. Here we go...

We got a new assistant manager about a year into my career at Lane Bryant. Let's call her Alexis. She was the quintessential bad girl: tall—like, eight feet tall—with a stern, tense face framed by the unsettling, partially grown-in stubble of her shaved eyebrows. While only twenty-one, she had the voice of a lifelong pack-a-day smoker (think Bea Arthur with a chest cold) and would tell long tales of growing up with her family on the Indian reservation near the local casino. She complained about anything and everything while twirling the creepy skull ring on her nicotine-stained finger.

She must've made at least three times what I did in her

high-up managerial position, but for some reason she inevitably asked me at the end of every shift to drive her to the bar across the river. Alexis and I couldn't have been more different, but I liked her, even though I knew she was trouble.

As we were closing down the store one night, I caught her putting some merchandise into her bag. "Just a little for me," she said, laughing as if it was no biggie.

I didn't dare say anything, knowing that (A) she was my boss and (B) she was stronger than me. I kept waiting for a blood-curdling alarm to go off as I walked out of the store that night next to Alexis and her bulging bag of concealed contraband, but nothing happened. Life just went on as usual.

A couple months later, I caught her stealing again. "Umm," I gathered the courage to say, "aren't you gonna get in trouble or something?"

"Please," she huffed, "there's so much crap here and they don't keep track of anything. You should take stuff, too, if you want."

As I retell this tale, I wish I had that famous DeLorean from *Back to the Future* so I could travel back in time. I'd drive right up to my younger self in the mall parking lot, roll down the window, and through a cloud of smoke yell, "Don't do it! Don't throw your whole life away!"

But back then I just wanted Alexis to like me. She was my superior, and she cursed even better than my dad's friends.

"I don't know. I mean, this is all girl's stuff."

Alexis reminded me, "You said that you liked those pajama bottoms with the gray stripes. They're kinda manly. Totally unisex."

She was right. They *could* look good on me, even if they were made to be worn by a soccer mom with a sweet tooth. They were a little manly. Maybe that was why they weren't selling. I mean, they were already marked down 40 percent. Nobody would miss them, right? They can't give these things away. I was kinda doing the company a favor!

"I guess they *could* be cute." I was torn. I hadn't purposely done anything this wrong since I was six years old at Expo '86, when I deliberately stomped on a mustard packet on the ground, splattering the white jeans of a little girl in front of me in bright yellow. I don't even know why I did it, but when that little girl burst into tears and her mother shot me a look of utter contempt, I felt so, so bad. Much like the mustard on her white jeans, the guilt of that moment has stayed with me forever.

With that feeling in mind, I knew stealing the pajamas was wrong, but it wasn't going to result in anyone bursting into tears, right? This was kind of a victimless crime. Besides, Alexis did this kind of thing all the time, and nothing *ever* happened to her. Looking back, of course, I was clearly trying to justify it, but that's what you do when you're doing something you shouldn't be doing.

It was a stupid risk, the wrong thing to do, the kind of act my grandma would call "a bonehead move," but I did it anyway. I slipped the PJs into my bag and walked out like nothing was wrong, just as I had seen Alexis do so many times before.

The funny thing is, I didn't even really want those pajamas. I tried to wear them that night, but was too wrought with guilt. In an attempt to push the entire mess out of my mind, I balled them up and hid them in the bottom drawer of my dresser. But I knew they were there—I couldn't forget them. They haunted me like an annoying tune that gets stuck in your head for days at a time, only this time the song was *Bad boy, bad boy, whatcha gonna do? Whatcha gonna do when the PJ police come for you?*

About a week later, I got a call to come in to work on my day off. *Awesome,* I thought, *I could use some extra hours.*

When I arrived, my boss Kend'rah greeted me, looking less spunky than usual. Even her hair was flat today. I asked, "What's wrong, honey?"

With a forced, sad smile, she replied, "There's a man in back. He needs to see you right away."

My heart sank. I didn't know if I was more upset about what I was about to endure or the look of disappointment on Kend'rah's face.

I walked slowly toward the back room and found a bald, stocky man in a dark blazer sitting among the empty cardboard boxes and hangers. "Please take a seat," he said curtly while gesturing to the folding chair opposite him.

I sat. My knees shook. I knew what was coming.

He maintained steady, almost creepy eye contact while he introduced himself. "I'm with corporate, Ross. I run the theft department. I'm here for a couple reasons. First, I need you to know that Alexis was fired today. She's been stealing."

I nodded.

"And I want to ask you something," he continued. "What would you say if I told you that we had video surveillance of you leaving this store with items that belonged to our company?"

I gulped.

"I need you to be honest with me, Ross."

I felt like shit. I had *really* screwed up. This wasn't me. I wasn't the guy who got caught stealing things and had to sit across from scary bald guys and admit embarrassing mistakes. I was better than this. Yes, I had made the absolute wrong decision. The only thing to do now was to man up and admit it.

"I took a pair of pajamas. They're in a drawer in my bedroom. I don't know why. I've never done anything like this before and I'm so, so sorry."

He let me leave without calling the authorities, but I had to return the pajamas. I also had to turn in my employee card and my official Lane Bryant name tag. It was like one of those scenes in a movie where they fire a rogue cop who's crossed over to the dark side and he's forced to hand in his badge and gun. Totally sad.

So, let me give you the one-line CliffNotes version of my confession: I was fired for stealing discount elastic-waist ladies' pajamas from a store for plus-sized women. Does it get any lower than that? I didn't just hit rock bottom, I hit rock pajama bottom.

I've lived with the shame of this pajama-clad skeleton in my closet for far too long. Forget the PJs. The real crime here—what I am most disappointed about—is the fact that I betrayed myself in order to seem cool. I went against my gut feeling, my gut that was twisting and turning in an attempt to tell me, *Don't do this! Just because someone else got away with it doesn't mean it's okay! You know better than this!*

I not only lost a job I loved that day, I lost my self-respect.

And I have since vowed to make choices that ensure I never feel that way again.

Now that I've confessed, I don't expect forgiveness. But I do hope, in the deepest depths of my heart, for two simple miracles: One, I hope my mother isn't too disappointed in her "perfectest little angel face." And, two, I hope some-day that the fine people at Lane Bryant corporate could find in their hearts to wipe my record clean and maybe, just maybe, welcome me back into their corporate family with open arms.

Perhaps we could even have a pajama party. Too soon?

Chapter Nine

HOW I BECAME BFFS WITH OSCAR WINNER GWYNETH PALTROW

D o you believe in besties at first sight? I sure do. Why? Because I was BFFs with Oscar-winning actress Gwyneth Paltrow a full six years before I even met her. Let me explain.

She first appeared on my radar in 1996 when Brad Pitt thanked her at the Fifty-third Annual Golden Globe Awards after he won Best Supporting Actor for *12 Monkeys*, which I very much enjoyed even though I somehow missed the first eleven.

Now, I can't remember my ATM PIN number or where I park my car at Home Depot (luckily, a kindhearted lesbian always helps me find my way), but I will never, *ever* forget the first time I laid eyes on Ms. Paltrow. I was in my parents' living room, surrounded by my signature awards show buffet: Sour Patch Kids, Cool Ranch Doritos, and Mr. Pibb (it tastes just like Dr. Pepper at a fraction of the cost!).

When they cut to her in the audience, my heart skipped a beat. "Now *that's* my kind of lady," I thought to myself, licking precious Dorito dust from my fat fingers.

She looked breathtaking in a black-and-white sleeveless gown, her hair swept back in a sleek side part with a low bun. She was heavenly, yet down to Earth. A superstar, but totally approachable. The Goddess Next Door, you know what I mean?

Between you and me, I just YouTubed that particular Golden Globes moment again to relive the memory (and for fact-checking purposes) and, unlike presenter Alicia Silverstone, who resembled an extra on *Buffy the Vampire Slayer*, Gwyneth's look was timeless and still stands up today. I mean, come on, she's perfection!

From that moment on, I was obsessed. I eagerly gathered every tidbit of information on her I could find. Had I spent even half the time on school-related activities that I did studying Gwyneth 101, I could've sold more candy bars than anyone else in the school orchestra instead of that uppity bitch Maggie Lindstrom, who totally cheated because her dad bought, like, four whole boxes (karma's a bitch, Maggie, and all the candy bars in the world won't buy you an Oscar-winning best friend!).

What was I talking about? Oh yeah, my perfectly healthy obsession with a woman I'd never met...

Seriously, I don't want you to get the wrong idea. I didn't have a creepy shrine with a collage of cut-out pictures of Gwyneth surrounded by candles or anything. First of all, that would be plain ol' weird. And second of all, my mom would never let me burn candles in my room. I did, however, convince my friend Becky to record the following as my outgoing voice-mail message:

"Hi, you've reached Ross's phone. He's not here right

now, so leave a message after the beep. By the way, this is his best friend, Gwyneth Paltrow." *BEEP!*

I just knew that Gwyneth and I would eventually meet in real life and become the best of friends. I'm sure everyone thought I was crazy, but I was convinced that we'd be the biggest power couple since peanut butter and jelly.

Side note: I just had a PB and J last week for the first time in years, and let me tell you, there's a reason this combination is a time-tested classic. They are simply meant to be together, just like Gwyneth and me.

Cut to March 2002. I had been on *The Tonight Show* for only a few months when I got my dream assignment: covering the red carpet at the *Vanity Fair* Oscar party. OMG. This was, like, a big freaking deal. Especially for someone as dorked out over awards shows as I've been my entire life.

I found myself smack-dab in the epicenter of entertainment on the night of the Academy Awards, and it was even more magical than I ever dreamed it could be. I met the biggest stars in Hollywood—everyone from A to Z, Angelina to Zellweger. And just when I thought my life couldn't get any better, it *totally* did!

Suddenly, out of the corner of my eye, I saw her. The oxygen was sucked out of my lungs and the ground fell out from beneath my rented tuxedo shoes as I attempted to make sense of the glowing vision before me. The rest of the world instantly became silent, nothing but a blur of flashbulbs reflecting off sequined gowns, loaned diamonds, and the golden muscles of giant Oscar statues. Of all the red carpets in all the world, she had to walk onto mine. There she was: the peanut butter to my jelly, Miss Gwyneth Paltrow.

I watched breathlessly as she made her way down the press line, kindly stopping to give quick interviews with other reporters and correspondents. The closer she got to me, the more nervous I became. It was official—after years spent dreaming of the moment we'd finally meet and our lifelong friendship would begin, it was happening.

There were so many ways this could go down, and all but one was horrible. What if she just dismissed me, passing by with a patronizing nod? What if I shut down, exactly like I had nearly a decade earlier during my big moment with Tiffani-Amber Thiessen (see chapter 7)? Or the very worst possibility: she could be a total fucking bitch.

We've all heard horror stories of someone's idol toppling from their lofty pedestal, their sweet public image shattering into a thousand pieces with a single sneer or careless word. And what's left behind our heroes as they sashay to the next photo op? A road paved with resentment and littered with the broken hearts of disappointed fans.

I was worried that I, too, might be abandoned on that lonely road. I mean, I'd built Gwyneth up so much that anything other than her total commitment to be my new best friend would translate into utter rejection in my mind. Looking back, I realize my expectations for Fantasy Gwyneth were so high that the Real Gwyneth was pretty much stepping into a no-win situation. But guess what? Despite the odds, she won. She won my heart.

What happened next is so amazing, that I don't need to embellish it in any way. I offer it to you, dear reader, unadorned, exactly as it happened, in script form. I am doing this because I am convinced that this will one day be a scene in a movie of the week on Lifetime Television for Women (and gay men).

And please do not argue with your friends over who gets to play Gwyneth and who has to play me. I suggest you cast the roles based on body type and/or hair color.

EXT. VANITY FAIR OSCAR PARTY AT MORTON'S, WEST HOLLYWOOD

(OSCAR WINNER GWYNETH PALTROW, RADIANT IN AN ALEXANDER McQUEEN GOWN, IS BEING USHERED PAST THE EQUALLY RADIANT TV CORRESPONDENT ROSS MATHEWS, DRESSED IN HEAD-TO-TOE MEN'S WAREHOUSE. "YOU'RE GONNA LOVE IT—WE GUARANTEE IT." AS SHE PASSES, HE YELLS.)

ROSS

Gwyneth! Please make a dream come true and talk to me!

(GWYNETH BREAKS AWAY FROM THE USHER'S VISELIKE GRIP TO TURN TOWARD THE WOMAN SHE HEARS YELLING. A BRIEF LOOK OF CONFUSION PASSES ACROSS HER FACE WHEN SHE SEES THAT THE SHOUTING EMITTED FROM ROSS. IT IS QUICKLY REPLACED BY A SMILE OF RECOGNITION.)

OSCAR WINNER GWYNETH PALTROW

I know who you are! You're hilarious!

ROSS

You do NOT know who I am!

OSCAR WINNER GWYNETH PALTROW

I do! I've seen you on "The Tonight Show"!

(ROSS LETS OUT A PRIMAL, GUTTURAL, ANIMAL-LIKE SHRIEK.)

ROSS

Then hug me and pretend like you know me!

(GWYNETH MOVES IN WITHOUT HESITATION AND PULLS ROSS INTO A WARM, FAMILIAR EMBRACE, THE KIND OF EMBRACE ONLY SHARED BY TWO PEOPLE WHO HAVE KNOWN EACH OTHER IN SEVERAL PAST LIVES.)

ROSS (Cont.)

Will you be my best friend?

(SHE REPLIES ALMOST BEFORE HE HAS FINISHED ASKING THE QUESTION.)

OSCAR WINNER GWYNETH PALTROW

Yes!

(ONE BY ONE, JADED JOURNALISTS AND CYNICAL CELEBRITIES ALIKE BEGIN TO SLOWLY APPLAUD,

ECHOING ACROSS THE RED CARPET, EVENTUALLY BUILDING TO A DEAFENING ROAR OF APPROVAL. GWYNETH LIFTS A JUBILANT ROSS ONTO HER SHOULDERS, AND AS THEY TRIUMPHANTLY RUN INTO THE VANITY FAIR PARTY, A LA THE CLIMACTIC ENDING OF ANY CHEESY 1980S MOVIE THAT WE'VE ALL SEEN A THOUSAND TIMES, THE MOMENT ENDS IN A HEART-WARMING FREEZE FRAME.)

END CREDITS ROLL OVER DIONNE WARWICK'S
"THAT'S WHAT FRIENDS ARE FOR"

FADE TO BLACK

Okay, so that last part didn't really happen. The crowd didn't applaud, and Gwyneth didn't lift me onto her shoulders (not that she couldn't have, the woman does Pilates!). But everything else, I shit you not, is all freakin' true! Gwyneth Paltrow seriously just agreed to be my best friend, and she did it on camera for the whole world to see! That would hold up in any court in the land!

After our legally binding friendship was agreed upon, she asked me for my e-mail address and I gave it to her, along with my cell phone number and my dorm phone number and my mom's phone number and... What can I say? I wanted to cover my bases. I remember how badly my hands were shaking as I wrote down my contact information for Gwyneth, scribbling every bit of personal information, short of my blood type. She gently took it from me and kept it in her hand. You can actually see it in publicity photos taken that evening.

As we continued chatting, our undeniable connection was beginning to draw a crowd. Everyone seemed fascinated by our giddy, schoolgirl exchange. It was clear to all present that they were witnessing the birth of a legendary friendship. Eventually, we parted ways, and she continued down the red carpet and into the party. It was hard letting her go, but almost poetic, like releasing a beautiful dove back into its natural habitat.

When I finally got home around 2 a.m., I felt just like Cinder-fella returning from the ball. *Is this a fairy tale?* I asked myself. I had not only met but also had an amazing conversation with the very person whose face was now staring back at me from posters and magazine clippings on my dorm room wall. *Nuts.*

I immediately checked my voice mail—which, by the way, still featured my friend Becky's faux Gwyneth outgoing message—but there was no call from the real thing (yet).

Cut her some slack, I thought to myself. *Gwyneth is probably still rubbing elbows with the crème de la crème of Tinseltown.*

I had to share the amazing news with someone, but it was definitely way too late to call my mom. So I did the only thing I could think of—I awoke my roommate and best friend Ryan by screaming these three words directly into his peacefully sleeping face: *"I MET GWYNETH!!!"*

By the next morning, I had recounted the story at least a hundred times to anyone who would listen and they all had the same question: "Do you think you'll actually hear from her?"

And my answer was always a grateful, "I dunno, but honestly, she's given me so much already, I could die a happy boy even if we never see each other again."

But that was a total lie. It was torture. Even though logic told me that a megastar like her reaching out to someone like me was a long shot, I constantly checked my e-mails and voice mails, and I picked up the phone every few minutes just to make sure it was working. I was still on cloud nine from our magic moment the night before, but I quickly came to terms with and accepted the fact that even though we had what I thought was a real connection, I would probably never hear from her again. You know those Hollywood types—they're "busy," which, of course, is French for "flaky." I had all but given up.

That next morning, I was about to head out to the dining hall to drown my sorrows in a breakfast burrito the size of a newborn baby when something told me to check my e-mail one last time. And, you guys? OMG, there was *one* unread e-mail.

"Please God," I prayed, "Let this not be an ad for penis enlargement or spam from a Nigerian Prince needing help to transfer his fortune from an overseas account."

I took a deep breath and clicked on Inbox. There it was—*the* e-mail.

Again dear reader, there is no need to gild the lily or put an artistic spin on this. Would you throw glitter on the Declaration of Independence or add a fart joke to the script for *Steel Magnolias*? No, you wouldn't. And I wouldn't dare change even one word of Gwyneth's first e-mail to me. I offer it to you now, in all its simple, pristine beauty:

Mon., March 25, 2002

Hello, it's Gwyneth. Very nice to meet you last night. Is this the right address for you? Verify before I continue or say anything too risqué.

xo, gp

Umm, what?!? Are we having an earthquake?!? Am I having a stroke?!? Did I just accidentally smoke some black tar heroin?!? Pinch me, smack me, punch me in the face. This. Cannot. Be. Real.

Needless to say, I e-mailed her back faster than you can say *Shakespeare in Love*!

For the next few days we traded revealing e-mails back and forth, each of us giving the other a crash course in our backgrounds—everything from boys to parents to careers to fashion. In other words, pretty much everything that matters between a straight girl and her new gay bestie. You've heard the phrase *fast friends*? This was speed of light! And it was *fantastic*!

I was so wrapped up in our newfound friendship, I almost completely forgot that my brand-new pen pal was a bona fide superstar. I felt so at ease with her, but why? Maybe it was because I felt so comfortable behind the safety of my computer screen? Maybe it was because I had always been convinced we'd be friends if we ever met? Or maybe, just maybe, it was because part of me didn't believe the e-mails were actually from Gwyneth at all.

A little voice in my head was pestering me, whispering, *Psst! Hey, moron! This is too good to be true! Did it ever occur to you that maybe someone is playing a cruel trick?*

Oh no. Perhaps that cruel voice inside my head was right and some jealous journalist, having witnessed our love fest the night before, had decided to screw with me? Yep, as much as I wanted to believe my friendship with Gwyneth was genuine, I had to admit that the more plausible explanation was that this was all some kind of cruel joke. Things like this just didn't happen to normal people like me!

As the months went by, this suspicion festered and grew into a full-blown conspiracy theory. After six months of nurturing an intimate friendship with either Oscar winner Gwyneth Paltrow or a designer-imposter Gwinyth Paltroh, I decided it was time for me to either finally meet my new best friend in person or call the bluff of the most heartless prankster in the history of the world. I took a brave step and asked her to lunch.

Regardless of which Gwyneth—fake or real—showed up, this meeting was technically my very first Internet date. Accordingly, my outfit choice was of paramount importance. After much consideration, I opted for Gap jeans in a medium wash, paired with an extra-large gingham print dress shirt in bubblegum pink. It was a look that said, *I'm friendship material and, more important, I'm not afraid of color.*

The location for lunch was ladies' choice and she recommended the Ivy in Beverly Hills. I'd never heard of it, but once I arrived I quickly realized that it was paparazzi central and *totally* fancy. If this was indeed a faux-Gywneth, they had done their homework. I had to tip my hat to their attention to detail, as this place was spot-on. I approached the maitre'd and shyly muttered, "I'm here for...um, the reservation's under...um...Gwyneth Paltrow?"

He glanced down from his podium and responded, "Ms. Paltrow hasn't arrived yet, sir."

I stood there and waited, taking in the ambience and trying not to eavesdrop on the well-known dining patrons, including agents and starlets (all of them ignoring the baskets of bread on their tables). I took advantage of the time spent waiting, taking a few precious minutes to remind myself that I deserved to be there, that I was worthy. Moments later, I looked up and saw a blonde vision approaching. It was the real deal, Ms. Gwyneth Paltrow, in the flesh.

My first thought? *HOLY SHIT! THERE'S GWYNETH PALTROW!*

My second thought? *HOLY SHIT!!! SHE'S HERE TO SEE ME!!!*

What a weird feeling, you guys. The only way I could describe it is like this: pretend you're at the Louvre seeing the Mona Lisa for the first time, and you're like, "Oh my God, it's the actual Mona Lisa!"

How cool, right? But while you're still freaking out over that mind-blowing fact, the security guards take the painting off the wall and hand it to you. It was *beyond* surreal.

Gwyneth approached me, her arms opened wide, "Ross!"

I couldn't even reply. I was still kind of in shock while we hugged. As she squeezed me tight, she continued, "It is so good to see you! Are you hungry? Let's eat!"

Fame *and* food? She really *was* the perfect woman.

Gwyneth and I were seated at our table and began looking over our menus. She looked even more lovely than I had remembered. She had no makeup on, her hair was down and she was wearing flip-flops. She looked effortlessly ethereal, like your really pretty friend from junior high who just so happens to be a movie star. Still, I had first-date jitters and decided to come clean about it.

"I have to tell you," I said. "I'm feeling a little intimidated."

She seemed shocked. "Are you serious? You're intimidated by *me*? Why?!? We've been e-mailing for months."

"I know, but it's different in person. I mean, this might sound dumb, but you're...Gwyneth Paltrow."

She cracked a reassuring smile, reached across the table, and put her hand on mine. "Give it ten minutes, you'll be over it."

And you know what? She was right. I hate to use the word *perfect*. I don't even know if "perfect" exists (the closest I've ever seen is Justin Timberlake in his music video for "Sexy Back"), but it's the only way I can think of to describe our lunch. We gossiped and laughed for hours—you know, like real friends do. The only difference was that, when we left, we had to sneak out the back to avoid the hordes of paparazzi that had camped out front after learning that she was there.

In the years since, our friendship has grown and continues to blossom. I've flown all the way to London to visit her, and we make a point to get together for dinner as often as possible when she's in Los Angeles. We also continue to e-mail on a regular basis, keeping each other up-to-date on our daily lives and also helping one another through life's challenges, most notably the loss of both our fathers just months apart. I can't speak for her, but when I lost my dad, she was the only friend of mine who had gone through the same experience and knew how that felt. Her support and insight were invaluable to me.

What started out as a mission to become very best friends with a version of a person I had created in my head has evolved into something entirely different and much deeper than what I had ever expected. Somewhere along the way, through birthday presents and broken hearts, shopping trips and shared meals, it stopped mattering to me that she's Oscar-winning actress Gwyneth Paltrow. Nope, that doesn't matter to me at all now. What does matter is that I just really, truly love her and she really, truly loves me.

So I have a message to all of you out there who dream of someday being BFFs with the one and only Gwyneth Paltrow. I know how you feel. I've been where you are. I've walked in your shoes. *But back off—the bitch is mine!*

Get your own Oscar-winning best friend. I hear Kate Winslet is available.

Chapter Ten

PRACTICALLY PAW-FECT IN EVERY WAY

As I sit here in my cozy little Los Angeles home, typing away on my laptop, I am flanked on either side by my favorite "laptops" of all: my precious pups, Louise and Mijo. Along with my partner, Salvador, we are a perfect family. It's hard for me to remember a time when we didn't wake up to these furry joyful faces, tongues hanging out beneath their big brown eyes, their tails wagging enthusiastically. I truly believe that destiny brought us all together. But to really tell the story of how this human-dog family came to be, we have to go back in time to a day before these two cuddly canines were even born.

Dogs are nothing new to me. I grew up in a family that loved big dogs. That's all we ever had—wonderfully large, floppy, slobbery canines. The first official Mathews pup was a Springer Spaniel. I know what you're thinking: *That's a large dog?!?*

But, come on, gimme a break. I was three years old and everything seemed big to me then. Her name was Bootsie, and because I was so young at the time, my only remaining memory of her is a photo taken of us when I had chicken pox. We were both covered in matching spots: hers brown, mine bright red. Adorable, right?

After Bootsie, we had Iggy, named after Ignatowski, my dad's favorite character on *Taxi* (played by Christopher Lloyd, best known as Doc Brown in the classic *Back to the Future*, the pretty good *Back to the Future 2*, and the crapfest *Back to the Future 3*).

Our dog Iggy was a big, strong golden Lab, and an expert hunter. Witnessing Iggy diligently deliver mallard after dead mallard to my father's feet left my dad's hunting buddies in awe. "Shit, Tom, you ol' cocksucker," they'd marvel, "that son of a bitch Iggy is the finest damned dog I ever did see."

They were right. Iggy really was the best. He must have weighed like a hundred pounds, and yet he'd purr like a tiny kitten when I'd pet him. I had such a great childhood with Iggy. While he gnawed on enormous *Flintstones*-sized soup bones out on our backyard patio, I used to sit on the other side of the sliding glass door with a dry erase board, trying to teach him English. I found it so frustrating that he couldn't speak and I yearned to know what he'd say if only he could. He'd stare attentively at me as I delivered my lecture. "A is for apple! A sounds like 'Aaaaaayyyyyy.' You like apples, don't you, Iggy? If you say it, you can have all the apples you want!"

This was pre–cell phone, or I would have the footage to prove it, but I swear one time he *almost* said it.

We truly had a soul connection, Iggy and I. He lived until the ripe old age of fifteen, when the agonizing pain in his hips finally took its toll. Dogs can never really let you know how much pain they're in, but you could see it in his eyes and almost feel it every time he tried to stand up. He was so much braver than I would have been. I'm such a drama queen—I get a sore throat and you'd think I was starring in the Broadway musical version of *Terms of Endearment* (mental note: tweet Tony winner Kristin Chenoweth about this). But not Iggy, he was strong.

Even though it was inevitable, putting him down was something my family constantly dreaded for the last few years of his life. But when the time finally came, the experience was actually quite beautiful, believe it or not. As he lay on the examining table at the vet's office, my entire family gathered around him, recounting our favorite Iggy stories and telling him over and over how much we loved him. The vet administered The Shot, and as our beloved Iggy drifted off into an eternal nap, gently dropping his head into my arms, we kissed him on his chocolate nose and said a final good-bye. I wish we could all go that way—gracefully and surrounded by love.

It was the first time in my young life that I'd ever experienced death. Initially, I was worried that the pain of Iggy's passing would scar me forever, making it impossible for me to even consider touching another K-9 with a ten-foot pole. But once a dog person, always a dog person, and by the time I was in college, I could no longer deny that I was, in fact, one of "those" people. I began to allow myself to daydream about my postcollege pet. I would graduate, move into an apartment, and get a dog of my very own.

I already had an inclination as to what this new puppy would look like: she'd be a she, and as small as she could be. Owning a small dog was a first for a Mathews man. As I mentioned earlier, I come from a long legacy of large-dog lovers. Historically, Mathews men measure their masculinity by the pounds of their pooches, but I was smart enough to know that ignoring lapdogs was a complete lapse in judgment.

Don't get me wrong: big dogs are wonderful. America's loved them for generations—Rin Tin Tin, Lassie, and the dog from *Turner and Hooch* (I can never remember which one was the dog and which one was Tom Hanks). If big dogs work for you, by all means, go adopt two or three right now and give them a wonderful life and a good home.

You've heard the phrase "Bigger is better"? But when it comes to dogs, at least, I personally couldn't disagree more. For me, it's less about "size" and more about "sighs" (as in, "*Ahhhhh! Oh my God, how cute is that scrumptious li'l dog?!?!?!?!?*").

Here are some arguments for why, in my opinion (and it's my book, so, not to be rude, but it's kinda the only opinion that matters right now), little dogs tower above their gargantuan counterparts. I have to warn you, I was on the debate team in high school, so you might want to skip this part if you don't want to be absolutely convinced that I'm right and you're so totally wrong.

- **Small dogs make traveling with a pet a breeze!**

Heck, one of literature's (and cinema's) most famous tiny terriers, Toto, accompanied Dorothy all the way to Oz. In real life, pint-sized pooches are so portable, they can easily and comfortably fit right beneath the seat in front of you. Ever seen a Standard Poodle in first class? I didn't think so, lady!

- **Small dogs make great dates!**

You can tote a teacup toy poodle with you pretty much anywhere: while watching a double feature at the movies, browsing organic beets at the farmers market, or leisurely enjoying the most important meal of the day, brunch. I can't imagine anything harder than trying to hide a Doberman Pinscher under a flimsy plastic patio table while discreetly feeding it nibbles of turkey sausage and simultaneously sipping bottomless mimosas. It's just not gonna happen, buddy!

- **Small dogs put the "fun" in "bodily *fun*ctions"!**

Have you ever looked at poop and thought to yourself, *Okay, now* that *is positively precious!*? Take it from me, a little doggie's doodie is ca-ca-cuuuute! Every teeny turd looks like a tiny Tootsie Roll! I've seen strangers struggle to use industrial-sized Hefty bags to pick up putrid piles of poo after their giant dog takes a mountainous dump. Yuck! Is that a dog or a horse? Get a shovel, honey!

- **Small dogs are so cute, they almost look fake!**

When I was a kid, I always wished my plush Pound

Puppy from Toys"R"Us would magically come to life
and hug me back. I named him Spanky, but for the life
of me I don't know why. What was I thinking?!? I'd
love to know where my head was back then. "Spanky"
sounds *very* S&M, which is *so* not me (unless you
blow a kiss my way during happy hour—I mean, who
doesn't bust out the faux-fur covered handcuffs after a
few too many two-for-one Mai Tais, am I right or am
I right?). Anyhoo, Spanky never did return my affec-
tions, and I still crave it to this day. So whenever I
come upon a little dog, I can't help but see a living,
breathing stuffed animal—just like that toy I had always wished would cuddle me back. Okay, okay...I
see that look on your face. What? I bravely open up to
you about my childhood need for companionship, and
you have the audacity to *judge* me? Learn to love, asshole!

• **Small dogs have big hearts!**

While all dogs offer unconditional love and faithful
devotion, which would you rather have sitting on your
chest while fighting the flu or a nursing a wicked hang-
over (damn those discount Mai Tais!)—a massive Pit
Bull or a mini Pomeranian? Like Snoopy himself, small
breeds offer an endless supply of healing and sweet
kisses that can soothe every Charlie Brown situation,
from unrequited love to failure on the football field.
Good grief, Lucy!

- **Small dogs are good in bed!**

    Gross! That's not what I meant and you know it, perv! What I'm saying is that they don't take up as much room in bed as big dogs do. Although you'd be surprised at what a shameless mattress hog an eight-pound Maltese can be. How is that even possible, by the way? Seriously, it defies science. Still, it's better than a king-sized Setter on a queen-sized Serta. If you don't believe me, go ahead and try to count sheep with a sheet-stealin' sheepdog. Sweet dreams, sister!

- **Doggy Style is awesome!**

    Jeez, you really need to get your mind out of the gutter! I'm talking about the most irrefutable selling point of all to raising a little dog: *you can dress them up!* Fido fashion is fresh, fearless, and infinitely fun. Black tie, business casual, sports gear, Western wear—the outfit possibilities for a small dog are endless (trust me on this, because I've explored them all). Check out your local Petco, people. Think about it: when was the last time you saw a simply sensational sundress and sassy sunflower sombrero made to fit a sixty-seven-pound Saint Bernard? Exactly—it doesn't exist. I don't make the rules, I just blindly follow them. Gnaw on that, numbskull!

By now, I'll assume you're thoroughly convinced and have enthusiastically jumped aboard the Small Dog Express. *Toot toot!*

For me, the case was clear. A little dog was the way to go. Unfortunately, pets weren't allowed in the small apartment I lived in after college, which was a shame, because it was only a few hundred dollars a month and had relatively few cockroaches (probably because the rats ate them). The decision was simple: I had to find somewhere else to live—a place where wagging tails were welcome, drinking out of the toilet bowl wasn't a crime, and man's best friend was considered an acceptable roommate.

You know when the universe gives you exactly what you need, exactly when you need it? Like finding a $20 bill in your pocket when you're broke and your gas tank is empty, or when Christina Aguilera's "Genie in a Bottle" comes on the radio when your spirit is broken and your soul is empty. Just like that, finding my next apartment proved to be one of those cosmic, meant-to-be kind of things.

Driving to the craft store one day, I took a wrong turn down a side street and got lost. When I pulled into a driveway to turn around, I almost hit a For Rent sign that read: 2 Bedroom, 1 Bath, Fenced Backyard, Pets Welcome.

Pets welcome? A backyard? *Craft store adjacent?!?* Where do I sign?!?

Five minutes after I'd completed the paperwork and the place was officially mine, Operation Find Fido was in full swing. I told everyone I came in contact with to keep an eye out for the perfect dog. I left no stone unturned, reaching out to every person I knew—from my butcher, to my baker, to my candlestick maker.

Everyone in my life knew I was looking for my doggie soul mate, Louise. Yes, Louise. It was preordained, that would

be her name. Why Louise, you ask? Five simple reasons:
One, it's a beautiful name. Two, three, and four, Louise is
the middle name of my mother, my grandmother, and my
great-grandmother. And five, on the rare occasions when my
precocious puppy misbehaved at the dog park, I could sing
out, "Geez, Louise!" while racing after her.

Almost as soon as the search party started, we struck
gold. I got a call from a friend who was nearly hyperventilating with excitement. "Ross, I was just at the vet's office
where I saw the most amazing, teeny-tiny, fluffiest thing you
could ever imagine. I think I might have found your Louise."

I dropped everything and raced to my prospective new
dog-ter's side.

It turns out that a rescue organization had just saved a
mom and her litter, consisting of three four-week-old puppies, from a cement pipe in a vacant lot amid the mean
streets of South Central Los Angeles. Each teeny pup
weighed no more than a pound and looked like an oversized
ball of cotton. I rushed to meet them, and the instant I held
the little girl puppy, fitting perfectly in the palm of my hand,
she had me in the palm of hers.

Yep, I was wrapped around her little finger, which of
course wasn't really possible because she's a dog with paws,
but you get my point. She was the most precious, beautiful
creature I'd ever seen. Obviously intelligent and inquisitive,
she kept constant eye contact as I spoke to her. Her fur
was softer than a fancy store-bought teddy bear, her puppy
breath was the sweetest thing you've ever smelled (mark
my words, whoever figures out how to bottle the scent of
puppy breath and sell it on QVC will be a billionaire), and

her chocolate-brown nose was exactly the same size as a Gummy Bear's head.

I knew, without a doubt, I was finally meeting her, the Louise I'd been yearning for. And you know what? I was right. She was, and still remains, the most paw-fect little doggie angel face I've ever met. Well, she used to be the sole carrier of that title, but now she happily shares it with a four-pound Chihuahua named Mijo.

Fast-forward about five years. Louise is a vivacious, grown-up lady with two daddies: me and my partner, Salvador. Side note: in my next life I want to come back as the pampered pooch of two doting gay men. Can you say "center of attention"?

We had just returned from an Alaskan cruise and were positively exhausted. Starving and faced with an empty refrigerator, we did what all good same-sex couples do when short on food: we went hunting. Yep, we went hunting for artisanal cheeses and organic vegetables at our local farmers market.

Salvador knew the farmers market was one of my very favorite places. I love the neighborhood feel, the fresh produce, and, best of all, stopping to visit the doggies available for adoption. I'd been bugging him for months about the idea of adding to our family. "What do you think about getting another dog?" I'd often ask. "Don't you think Louise deserves a little brother or sister?"

But Salvador always insisted that it was a bad idea. As much as I persisted, there was simply no changing his mind. That was why I was so shocked that day at the farmers market when, while passing the adoptable pooches on our way out as we had done every Sunday before, he pointed at—no joke—the smallest dog I had ever seen and matter-of-factly said, "That one."

"Huh?" I was so confused.

"Look at that one. He's, I don't know...so cute. There's just something about him."

I'm not kidding you, the dog he was pointing at was less than half the size of the handmade chicken tamale I had just devoured while browsing for locally grown brussels sprouts.

The woman running the adoption agency approached us, smiling. "Do you wanna meet this little guy?" she asked while picking him up and placing him in Salvador's already outstretched arms.

I started squealing and clapping, knowing it was a done deal. He went home with us that very night and we named him Mijo (a Spanish term of endearment meaning "my son"). From the moment we welcomed him into our casa, he and his big sis, Louise, have been inseparable.

Which brings us back to me, sitting here on the couch in LA, bookended by the best two friends a guy like me could ever hope for. These two dogs—combined—weigh a mere twelve pounds, but their impact on our lives has been immeasurable. Sure, one day Salvador and I hope to have human kids of our own, but until we hear the pitter-patter of little feet, we're happy with the *clickity-clack* of paws with claws.

You see, the four of us are a family. Not only have they fulfilled my lifelong dream of being a doggy daddy to pint-sized pups, but they have also taught both Salvador and me so much. Louise came along right after my dad died and showed me that there can once again be joy after tragedy.

Mijo helped teach Salvador a whole new level of unconditional love. And they both taught us a valuable lesson all parents should know: if you have dogs or children and you're going to invest in expensive, high-quality, wall-to-wall carpet for your living room, avoid choosing a light color. May I suggest a deep dark brown? Trust me on this—no matter how hard you scrub, club soda doesn't get *everything* out.

Chapter Eleven

MALE BONDING

I know for a fact that I do not look good in camouflage. Who does? All those boring colors mixing together in an effort to blend in with your natural surroundings? As if! I'm no wilderness wallflower! No, I pick out my clothes with the sole intent of standing out. 'Cuz honey, if you've got it, don't camouflage it, camou-*flaunt* it! Besides, if I wanted to spend my days dressed in nothing but head-to-toe khaki and olive green, I would've become a Girl Scout (not a good idea—not only can I not start a campfire, but I'm not to be trusted around all those delicious cookies).

You should know by now that I would never dislike something without at least trying it first (need I remind you about my high school girlfriend, Carrie?). So, trust me when I tell you that camouflage is not my thing. I can talk the talk because I've walked the walk. And I did it in camouflage rubber hip-wader boots and matching waterproof jacket, accentuated with a red plaid Elmer Fudd cap.

Duck hunting was one of my dad's passions. He loved the outdoors, the quality camaraderie of male bonding, and the thrill of the hunt. As a youngster, I'd always watch as he and my brother left for a day of tracking down defenseless ducks. As he loaded up the truck with duck decoys, boxes of ammunition, and a couple cases of Schmidt's beer, my dad would pat me on the head and say, "Sorry, Rocky, you're too young. Maybe in a few more years."

I would feign disappointment, but was always secretly thrilled that I could just stay inside our warm and cozy house with my mom instead, helping her bake banana bread and learning how to properly load and unload the dishwasher. Eventually, the day came when I was old enough, at the ripe old age of eight, to accompany my dad out into the hunting fields.

"Put this on," he said, tossing me a camouflage jacket two sizes too big.

I did as he said, slightly honored that I was being included and slightly mortified by just how horribly unflattering the jacket was. But, even at that young age, I knew that this was a rite of passage in our family and I wanted to make my dad proud, even at the risk of looking unfashionable.

I spent the better part of our outdoor adventure shivering in the tall grass of a duck blind snacking on mini powdered doughnuts and Slim Jims while reading my *Little House on the Prairie* book, nonchalantly glancing upward to see if the shotgun blast ringing in my ears had resulted in a bloody duck plummeting from the sky.

While they were killing defenseless animals, I couldn't help but feel like I was a real buzzkill. So, in an attempt to impress my dad and his hunting buddies, I decided to finally stop dragging my feet, pull my nose out of the book, and just pull the trigger, literally.

The shotgun was heavier than I thought it would be, but I liked holding it, even though it was about as long as I was tall. I felt manly, like Kevin Costner in *Dances with Wolves*, only my movie would have been called *Prances with Puppies*. The only other time I had held a gun was at the county fair, but that gun was plastic and shot water at a tiny clown's mouth.

As I struggled to lift his gun to my shoulder, my dad watched, beaming with pride. "Okay," he whispered. "Close one eye and just use the scope to aim. Steady...Now, slowly pull the trigger."

I closed my eyes and held my breath as my chubby little finger squeezed the trigger. The violent kickback from the rifle resulted in two unexpected things: a nasty bruise on my shootin' shoulder, and a high-frequency scream from yours truly echoing across the countryside. Not exactly the effect I was going for. Needless to say, I renewed my library card, but not my hunting license.

Fishing, however, was more my cup of tea. I quite enjoyed the fresh air, the serene, soothing sounds of the water and, most of all, the stop-off at 7-Eleven on the way to the lake (fish may eat earthworms, but I have always preferred the gummy variety). Some of my favorite father-son memories revolve around those quiet moments floating on a lake in a minuscule metal dinghy of a boat, my dad sitting in the back near the small, toylike motor, flicking cigarette ash into the lake. I loved watching him steer from where I was seated in the front of the boat on a makeshift chair made out of a spare lifejacket and an old red-and-white cooler filled with bologna, Shasta grape soda, and beer.

I would stare directly at the end of my fishing pole, waiting—sometimes for hours—to feel a jolt, and for the tip of the pole to jerk down suddenly toward the water, a sure sign that I'd hooked a big one!

I was actually quite adept at reeling in a fish. The trick is in the wrist. Once I'd spun the handle what seemed like a thousand times, the fish would begin to appear, blurry at first, but clearer and clearer as it rose to the surface. This was where my job ended and my dad's began. As fun and exhilarating as it was to hook a fish, I wasn't about to actually touch the slimy thing once it came out of the water. Eww.

My dad never complained about doing the dirty work. Instead, he would just roll up the sleeves of his flannel shirt, yank the hook out of the fish's mouth and whack it on the head with a wrench until it stopped wiggling. What a man.

On the rare occasions when we would encounter a dry spell while fishing, I never panicked. My dad taught me a surefire chant to beckon the fish that I'll never forget. After a few hours of unsuccessful fishing, he'd say, "Well, Rocky, I think it's time for the chant."

Without hesitation, I'd jump up in the middle of our little boat, forcing it to rock from side to side. Once I'd balanced myself, I'd look toward the heavens and shout the fishing chant my father had taught me: *"Rat shit bat shit dirty old twat! Thirty-seven assholes tied in a knot! Yay lizard shit!"*

Without fail, it always worked. I shit you not.

Oh, how I loved spending quality time with my dad. I savored those moments and yearned to find even more over which we could bond. My next attempt didn't just go well. In fact, you could say I scored a touchdown.

It might surprise you to know that, between manicures, happy hour, brunch, and watching makeover shows, I have had, since childhood, a hidden passion that takes up much of my time. So, what's my shocking secret? I'm a sucker for shoulder pads, and not just on my *Golden Girls*. Yes, believe it or not, I'm a *huge* football fan, just like any other normal red-blooded American boy!

I've been hut-hut-hikin' ever since I was a pint-sized pee-wee, watching football with my dad and brother every Sunday and Monday during the NFL season. Yeah, there's no doubt about it—we Mathews men really go hog wild for the ol' pigskin!

Are you surprised to hear I'm a fabulously fervent football fanatic? Don't be. I'm a very complicated person. I have more complexities than my delicious seven-layer dip, which always wins Most Valuable Player at my annual Super Bowl party buffet.

Watching and discussing football has just always been something I do, like brushing my teeth or improving every outfit I wear with a pair of brightly colored socks. It's just deeply ingrained in the fabric of who I am (and I'm not talking about a poly-cotton blend, people).

It kind of bugs me when people find out about my fondness for football and instantly assume, "Oh, Ross, you just watch because you like the beefy guys in tight pants."

That kind of knee-jerk gut reaction makes me want to knee those jerks in the gut! That's like saying straight men only watch professional figure skating to see the ladies in their skimpy outfits. That's ridiculous! I'll have you know that they watch figure skating for the sheer artistry of the sport, just like I do. Know what I mean? Or should I say, "Brian Boitan-know-what-I-mean"?

No, I happen to have a vast knowledge of the game of football itself. But to be perfectly honest, I fell in love with it by accident. As a kid, the real reason I gave football any attention at all was to spend time with my own personal MVP, my dad.

He simply *lived* for football, and by watching the games together, we found a mutual interest to bond over. For some strange reason, he wasn't into the things I was, like debating whether or not Dylan should choose Brenda over Kelly on *Beverly Hills 90210* or organizing Skittles by color.

So, with football as our common ground, I began rooting for my dad's favorite team, the Seattle Seahawks. Oh, our beloved Seahawks. Sure, they've rarely ever been any good, bless their hearts. Most years, any high hopes for Super Bowl championship glory are dashed by about the fifth game of the season when their record is usually something like a dismal 1-4, but still, we are the "twelfth man" (football term—look it up) and refuse to be fair-weather fans.

I used to daydream about growing up and becoming a player for the Seahawks one day. I imagined putting on my blue-and-green uniform with matching shoelaces and painting black stripes under my eyes. Not only would the stripes keep the glare of the bright stadium lights away, but they would also really accentuate my cheekbones. I'd sip on orange Gatorade with Steve Largent (#80 and my mom's *favorite* player) while trash-talkin' about the other team's poor hygiene and bad grooming habits until it was game time. And as I'd walk out onto the Kingdome field, I'd smile and wave to my dad, who'd be beaming with pride right in the front row at the fifty-yard line.

That would've been awesome, right? But as much as I loved watching sports, I was about as naturally athletic as a ceramic garden gnome. Despite limitations, I decided to take one for the team and give sports a try.

When I was about eight or nine years old, it was my dad's encouragement that led me to try T-ball, which is basically like softball with training wheels. As simple as the game was, I still sucked big time. Do you have any idea how embarrassing it is to spend an entire season wildly swinging a bat at a ball that's just sitting on a tee in front of you and striking out every single time? I do, and it's not fun.

It was even worse when the other team was up to bat. I'd just stand around in the outfield making dandelion necklaces while waiting for a pop fly that would never, ever come. You call that cardio? Please, I've burned more calories lounging on the couch while watching reruns of *Family Feud.*

There were nice moments, though, like Capri Suns and apple slices with peanut butter after each game. Also, we had some seriously dapper pinstriped uniforms that we bought after selling candy bars. And what I lacked in God-given athletic talent, I more than made up for in morale-boosting bravado. I mostly served as comic relief on the team, which I enjoyed because I felt *very* much like Rosie O'Donnell in *A League of Their Own.*

Next, I tried my hand at soccer. I was slightly better at it than T-ball, but that's not saying much. Without a doubt, my favorite part of being on the soccer team was photo day. I loved ironing my team T-shirt and bleaching my shin guards and then jockeying for position in the team photo (I always wanted to be kneeling in the front row because that angle minimized my double chin).

My least favorite part, by far, was when we played scrimmage. Why? Three horrifying, soul-crushing, panic-inducing words: *Shirts vs. Skins.* If you're thinking to yourself, *Why is that so scary?* consider yourself lucky. We chipmunk-cheeked chubby chaps know all too well the humiliation involved in the public baring of our pasty and pudgy prepubescent torsos.

Huffing and puffing across a soccer field was one thing, but the mere thought of doing it as a "skin" with my fully exposed man boobs bouncing up and down like Dolly Parton during an earthquake was crossing the line. Fortunately, there are perks when your dad is the coach and he knows you have low self-esteem. Thanks to him, my jersey always stayed on.

I played soccer for five years and scored only one goal. Well, technically one goal, but I didn't really earn it, at least not in the traditional way. But, still, it totally counts.

It happened in the last quarter of the last game of my soccer career. The score was tied with mere seconds left. I was doing what I usually did during a game, feigning interest in the action at the opposite end of the field while counting down the minutes until our postgame party at Godfather's Pizza. Out of nowhere, the ball came barreling toward me at, like, a gazillion miles per hour. I looked left, I looked right, but there was nowhere to run. Before I could duck, the soccer ball hit me square in the chest, taking the breath right out of my lungs and knocking me flat on my back.

Mother Hubbard, that hurt! Before I could cry out in pain, I rolled into the fetal position just in time to witness something I had never seen before: a soccer ball, just touched by me, rolling directly into the opponent's goal. I had just accidentally scored the winning point. The crowd went wild.

The high of that moment gave me the confidence I needed to attempt playing my favorite sport of all, football. I had spent so many years up to that point watching the professionals do it in the NFL, and I hoped deep down that I could emulate what my heroes did. While my dad took me shopping to buy my very first protective cup, I couldn't stop thinking about the upcoming season with my eighth-grade junior varsity team. I just knew we'd have the kind of heart and camaraderie that could take us all to way to the playoffs. I fantasized about the big championship game and my fourth-quarter Hail Mary pass that would be the cherry on the sundae of our Cinderella season.

Unlike Cinderella and her glass slipper, however, football and I were not a perfect fit. I quickly learned that watching the game is very different from playing the game. I found that the only thing I hated more than tackling other players was being tackled. That shit hurt. And even though I perfected a show-stopping signature touchdown dance—that, sadly, I never got to use—I soon came to the realization that I made a much better cheerleader than I did a linebacker.

As much as I longed to be a professional Seattle Seahawk as a kid, it just wasn't meant to be. And, you know what?

I'm okay with that. I may not have ever made it into the end zone, but I know I made my dad proud by stepping out of my comfort zone. As long as you try, you're triumphant. You can still find me every Sunday in front of a TV, thinking of my dad as I root for my beloved Seahawks and checking the scores of the other games with the Sports Center app on my iPhone like a real man's man.

After some time, I've come to terms with the fact that the highlight reel of my football career will be limited to that one time I beat my brother at John Madden Football on the Xbox and showing off my killer Nerf spiral in the front yard with my friends. Which, by the way, I just did today. True story.

Chapter Twelve

UNCLE ROSS AND ANTI-DRUG

All right kids, enough fun and games. Gather 'round Uncle Ross, because things are 'bout to get real for a minute up in this bizz'ook. Sit down, 'cuz you just might overdose on a massive hit of life lessons and I'm the only dealer in town.

I want to make an important public service announcement about something that is no doubt affecting you or someone you know. It's an insidious danger that's lurking around every corner, at every park across the street from every school and has been featured in at least one "very special episode" of every sitcom since the dawn of time. I'm talking about the original bad girl herself, a lady that goes by the name of Mary Jane. She has many nicknames: the Pot, Grass, Weed, Reefer, Ganja, Chronic, Cannabis, Sticky Icky, Maui Wowie, Acapulco Gold, and the Devil's Lawn Clippings, just to name a few.

I'll be honest with you, dear reader. Even I—squeaky clean Mr. By-the-Book himself—couldn't resist being lured into the smoky web of the Wacky Tobaccy. Yes, I've danced the forbidden dance with the Pot many a time and, boy, can that lady move!

When I was younger, I used to think I'd never try drugs. I knew drugs were for losers like that one cousin of mine whose other poor choices included a rebellious haircut complete with spiky bangs, shaved sides, and a rat tail. A look that screamed, *Back off, I'm trouble! Hang out with me, and you'll end up gettin' a neck tattoo!*

Keep in mind, this was in the early 1990s, nearing the end of Nancy Reagan's Just Say No campaign. I was constantly bombarded with anti-drug messages, just like every other sixth grader across America. A huge part of this community outreach frenzy was an in-school Drug Awareness Resistance Education program, better known by the sassy street-smart acronym, DARE.

To a kid like me, DARE was kind of awesome. Real-life police officers came to our classrooms loaded with freebies like stickers, erasers, and pencils, each one emblazoned with DARE's bright red, graffitilike logo. These totally radical prizes were given out as rewards to those of us courageous enough to participate in the educational fun. And, boy did I participate!

I was the absolute best when it came to role-playing the variety of dangerous drug-related scenarios in front of the class. I would often portray the part of the Voice of Reason when we practiced different ways to handle the inevitable peer pressure. "I...I don't know, Melissa. I don't think doing drugs is a good idea. Why don't we all go to Jimmy's house instead? He's got a Super Nintendo and his mom always has Jeno's Pizza Rolls in the freezer."

As raw and utterly believable as I was as the Voice of Reason, I was even more powerful when I'd immerse myself in the dark, gritty role of the Sinister Tempter. "Hey guys," I'd mumble, shuffling across the multipurpose room with my hands in my pockets. "Homework sucks, am I right? I don't know about you, but I could really blow off some steam with a good rolled-up joint of a marijuana cigarette. You know what I mean? A nice, deep inhale of drugs? Well, I just happen to have an entire Ziploc sandwich baggie of the Pot right here in my fanny pack. I know narcotics are against the law and our parents and teachers will be disappointed if we do them, but who cares, man? Let's have a wild drug party."

The program culminated with a year-end graduation ceremony held in front of the entire school. I had been in the audience for the DARE graduations of sixth-grade classes before me and, frankly, was underwhelmed. Paper police badges were taped to the shirts of all the graduates, and everyone was served a tiny cup of ice cream. That was it?!? These kids fought for an entire year in your war on drugs and they're rewarded with a dinky Post-it note badge and a single scoop of vanilla? Where's the pageantry, the celebration, the chocolate sprinkles?

I approached my teacher with my own plans for a new-and-improved finale to our upcoming DARE graduation ceremony. "Just picture it," I implored her. "The entire class dressed in matching black-and-red DARE T-shirts, beatboxing in unison. The crowd begins to clap along to our cool, funky beat. Suddenly, I break away from the group, stepping forward into the spotlight and then...I begin to rap! I rap about drugs! I rap about drugs like no one's ever rapped about drugs before! It'll be sensational!"

I must've really sold her on it, because my teacher gave me full creative control. "Sure, Ross. Go for it. Whatever. You're in charge."

OMG. Do you know what that meant, you guys? I was going to be the star, director, producer, and choreographer. This was huge. I was basically a young Barbra Streisand, and this DARE assembly would be my *Yentl*. (Feel free to sing along, "Pothead, can you hear me...?")

Under my sure-handed guidance, my classmates and I rehearsed relentlessly for weeks. It was important to keep morale up among my backup performers, so I encouraged them to customize their DARE T-shirts. I myself opted for a tastefully simple yet elegant costume, pairing my T-shirt with a classic red mock turtleneck (to set off the color of the DARE logo and make it really pop), pleated khakis with a stylish half-inch cuff, argyle socks, and a brand-spankin'-new pair of penny loafers. Hot!

Cut to the day of the big DARE graduation assembly. All of the students performing in the show gathered for a final dress rehearsal. As the visionary in charge, I was meticulous, insisting on perfection. "Rodrigo, it's one-two-pivot-pivot, not one-two-three-pivot! We've been over this like a hundred times!"

I could tell my backup performers were getting restless, but I begged them to run through the rap just one last time. I'm not going to lie to you, it wasn't great. No, it was phenomenal! I came alive on that stage, each succinct rhythmic rhyme pouring from my very soul, echoing throughout the multipurpose room with such glory!

Don't be a fool
'Cuz drugs ain't cool!
Take it from me
Avoid P—O—T!
Prove you care
Only if you DARE!
We invite you to hang
With our drug-free gang!
'Cuz the way to go
Is to "Just Say No"!

Oh, and dear God, how I moved! I covered every inch of that stage, clapping, jumping, popping, 'n' locking like an overeager extra from one of my mom's *Sweatin' to the Oldies* VHS tapes! Richard Simmons would have been so proud.

Reaching the glorious climax of my routine, I threw myself into the final one-two-pivot-pivot when something... happened. Something horrible. I had spun with too much passion, miscalculated a turn, and had veered dangerously close to the edge of the stage. The floor that had once been securely beneath my penny loafers was suddenly gone.

Suspended in midair between the edge of the stage and the linoleum floor—a distance of over five feet—I didn't think of the impending injury to my body. Instead, I thought one thing and one thing only: *Oh noooo, the shooooow!*

And then...a sickening thud. In mere seconds, I had gone from a dazzling, magical rapping sensation to a mangled pile of pleated khakis and argyle socks.

At the emergency room, I was an inconsolable, sobbing mess. Not because my wrist was broken and my knee had nearly swelled to the size of one of those disturbingly huge pumpkins people in overalls grow and then show off on the covers of small-town newspapers. No, I was upset because I knew that less than three miles away, the show was going on without me and, to add insult to injury, with Rodrigo as the lead.

I was shattered, just another casualty chewed up and spit out by the voracious monster known as Show Business. You would think if I was ever going to turn to drugs, it would be then. But actually, it happened two years later.

The first time I tried the Pot was in the middle of my freshman year at the wrap party for my high school's production of the musical classic *Oklahoma!* I was in the chorus (I still remember my one and only line—"Oh you would, would ya?"). You'd think the natural high of a Rodgers and Hammerstein show would have been intoxicating enough, but I was jonesin' for more, and these musical theater thugs were only too happy to share their stash.

One puff and I lost my stuff. I became a one-man giggle factory, and business was boomin'! And not only was the Pot at the party good, but the food was *amazing*, too. For some reason, I just couldn't get enough! And the music was fantastic. I'd never really paid attention to the words in "All That She Wants" by Ace of Base, but it's actually a superdeep song.

Needless to say, I quite enjoyed my first foray into the Pot. I enjoyed it so much, in fact, that from then on I often found myself shamelessly dipping into my older brother's hidden supply (sock drawer, duh!). When I came home to an empty house after a long day of school and extracurricular activities, I'd light up, grab four or five after-school snacks, sink into the couch, and disappear into another episode of *Rikki Lake*. But eventually, as much as smoking the Pot made me feel cool and rebellious, both the novelty and my buzz wore off. I mean, yeah, it was fun, but it made me love food and hate homework even more than I already did. As a result, my grades were falling and my pants weren't. It was time to get my shit together. I had to quit the junk.

But, wouldn't you know it? Just as I was beginning to turn my life around, I was dragged right back into the seedy underbelly of the drug world when my brother suddenly noticed that the only thing in his sock drawer was socks. "Hey, Dickwad," he hissed at me under his breath in the living room, "replace the fucking weed you stole or else."

Fair enough. Along with my new sobriety also came a new sense of integrity. After all, I did steal his drugs. The least I could do was put on my big-boy panties, buy him some more of the Pot and finally wash my hands of the rough-and-tumble underground drug world once and for all. The only way to accomplish this was to do something I never thought I'd find myself doing: I had to do a drug deal.

Let's face it, drug deals weren't for kids like me. They were for down-on-their-luck hoodlums, weak-minded thrill seekers, and former child stars. But these are the dirty back roads you're forced to walk down when you dance with the Devil and smoke his lawn clippings.

So, I ventured into the bad part of town. Just like the rest of small-town America, the bad part of Mount Vernon, Washington, is near the railroad tracks next to the diner that sells biscuits and gravy (with real sausage in the gravy).

Wanting to look the part, I wore my version of a "druggie" costume—a backward baseball cap, an oversized filthy T-shirt, ripped jeans, and a bandana tied around my upper thigh. It occurs to me now that I looked much more like a chunky Punky Brewster.

I approached a kid who couldn't have been much older than me. He looked like the demon offspring of Kurt Cobain and Alanis Morrisette and he kept swatting his long greasy hair away from his forehead with his middle finger. I couldn't tell if he was flipping me off or just couldn't see through his Jared Leto–like bangs. He struck me as surprisingly angry-looking for someone with such unlimited access to marijuana. I remember thinking to myself, *When they inevitably turn my life into a movie, this character has to be called "Dealer Dude." Oh my God, the guy who plays Becky's boyfriend on* Roseanne *would be perfect for the part!*

"Dealer Dude" didn't seem to notice my hand shaking with fear as I held out a wad of crumpled dollar bills. Saying nothing, he reached into the flannel shirt tied around his waist, handed me a sandwich baggie of green buds, and shuffled away (exactly, by the way, as I had done as the Sinister Tempter in DARE).

I had survived my first (and last) drug deal. And now, once I handed over the Pot to my brother, I could leave the sordid drug world behind me once and for all!

After my momentary detour to the dark side, I returned to the anti-drug movement with the same fervor I had during my glory days of DARE. But this time I was armed with what they call street cred. Now that I'd walked the walk, talked the talk, and smoked the Pot, I had a newfound perspective that would add an invaluable yet invisible layer of depth to my mission. I found my calling in the Straight 'n' Narrows, an aptly named after-school program comprising the best and brightest sober students in our small county. The mission of the Straight 'n' Narrows was to perform at all the schools in the area, offering up lots of drug-free drama and healthy humor in the form of entertaining skits.

I heard about the Straight 'n' Narrows from my friend Aubrey, a soprano whom I'd gotten to know in our school's jazz choir. Aubrey was featured prominently in the Straight 'n' Narrows, most likely because her mother was the founder and director. During my drug days, Aubrey was constantly pushing to get me involved in their sober celebrations. I may not have been interested back then, but now that I'd kicked the junk, I was intrigued.

"Aubrey," I asked one day, "what exactly do you guys do at Straight 'n' Narrows?"

Her face lit up. "Omigosh, Ross! It's amazing. The Straight 'n' Narrows is all about merging theater, drug awareness, and abstinence education. We meet every Wednesday night at the alternative school. You know, where boys on parole and pregnant girls go to class? Anyway, we start with an improv game. Like, we sit in a circle and everyone has to say their name and a teenage temptation that starts with the same letter. So, for instance, I'd say something like, 'Aubrey, Angel dust!'"

I was definitely a little interested, but didn't want to commit to anything. I mean, Wednesday night was *Melrose Place* night. But I'm a real sucker for a word game. "So, like, I could say 'Ross, Reefer'?"

"Omigosh! Exactly! You're perfect for this!"

She did have a point. I really was perfect for this. Still, I wasn't convinced. "I don't know, Aubrey. I'm pretty busy..."

Then she really went in for the kill. "Aw, that's too bad, because we have those big tubs of Red Vines from Costco and we always order way, way too much pizza."

That manipulative little bitch. "Should we carpool?"

And so started my career as a Straight 'n' Narrows standout. It turned out to be even better than I'd imagined. At my first meeting, I landed a killer monologue about a five-year-old kid whose deadbeat mom was a hardcore pot addict. I have to say, I was impressed with just how cutting-edge this group of community crusaders actually was.

Just when I thought it couldn't get any better, Aubrey's mom clapped her hands and announced, "All right, my little thespian soldiers. It's time for Total Eclipse!"

The room exploded with excitement. I whispered to Aubrey through a mouthful of Pizza Hut Meat Lover's, "Hey, what's Total Eclipse?"

"Omigosh, Ross, it's the absolute best performance piece! I play the Girl, and the rest of you represent temptations that we teens all face on a daily basis. You each wear a T-shirt with a different danger written on it, like LSD or PCP or Shoplifting or whatever. It's all set to that song "Total Eclipse of the Heart," and you all dance around in a circle, each enticing me to dance with you, symbolizing the—"

"Okay, I get it, Aubrey," I interrupted her. "I'm in."

The only T-shirt left was Sex, which was actually fine with me. As an artist, I'm always looking to stretch myself (and in this case, I was also stretching the size Small T-shirt over my XL body). I was still a virgin, so it wasn't like I could pull from life experience. Instead, my inspiration came from a strange mix of what I imagined sexy to be, from the sweet, innocent chemistry between Jasmine and Aladdin to the trashy, softcore heavy petting I'd seen on late-night Cinemax.

Attempting to describe a dance this visceral is like trying to describe color to the blind, but I'll try: Imagine about fifteen teenage kids in a circle with Aubrey in the middle. As "Total Eclipse of the Heart" began to play, we each swayed like seaweed in the ocean, slowly back and forth. We took turns approaching Aubrey, who valiantly fought against the onslaught of our advances, our hands grabbing at thin air, our bodies spinning in a lustful frenzy.

First Cigarettes tried to burn her, but she courageously pushed him away. Then Gossip attempted to whisper an unfounded rumor into her ear, but she'd have no part of it. That was my cue. I approached her like an animal in heat. My hungry arms were outstretched, and my hips were suggestively undulating, shamelessly dry humping the air.

It's fair to say that my steamy character Sex totally eclipsed the inexperienced real me. To really express the push and pull of addiction, I lifted Aubrey into the air a la Patrick Swayze and Jennifer Grey in *Dirty Dancing*. Granted, I could lift her only a few inches off the ground (I've always had the upper body strength of a four-year-old girl), but still, it was quite a moment.

In the months that followed, we took our show on the road and performed in countless gymnasiums across the state.

My career with the Straight 'n' Narrows came to a screeching halt, though, when my secret, hard-livin' past finally caught up with me.

It happened at a local high school in the midst of yet another flawless, crowd-pleasing Total Eclipse routine. I was twirling with passion in my sweat-drenched, skin-tight, threadbare T-shirt featuring iron-on letters that spelled S-E-X across my heaving man boobs. After my turn trying to seduce Aubrey, I looked out into the audience and saw a face that somehow seemed familiar.

He seemed to know me, too. We locked eyes, but I couldn't place him. *Wait*, I thought. *Do I sit next to him in Driver's Ed? Or is he the kid who bags groceries at Food Pavilion? Wait, what's he doing now? Is he flipping me off? No, he's just brushing his greasy bangs away from his—OH MY FUCKING GOD IT'S DEALER DUDE!*

Any possibility that he perhaps didn't recognize me flew right out the gymnasium window when he suddenly stared me right in my guilty face and blatantly started smoking a phantom joint like some marijuana-mad mime. Busted!

And as if it wasn't bad enough that my less-than-sterling life choices could possibly mess up my future, I had just messed up the choreography!

The very next day I respectfully resigned from the Straight 'n' Narrows, making up some flimsy excuse. I couldn't risk my unsavory past rearing its ugly head to possibly taint this amazing anti-drug group with a drug-related scandal. So I quietly folded up my Sex T-shirt, placed it in a plastic Food Pavilion grocery sack, and left it on Aubrey's front porch—along with my teenage passion for philan-thropic dance.

You think I never would've touched the stuff again. But I did. Oh, I'm almost positive that I should just stop here and save myself any further embarrassment. But for you, dear reader, I will tell this story.

Most people will assure you that it's not possible to over-dose on marijuana. Even bona fide doctors with training and fancy medical degrees will say so. But let me tell you, I've been there.

It was Thanksgiving weekend of 2003. I had returned from college to spend the holiday back in my hometown, but it was certainly no vacation. My mother was down in Seattle at a special cancer hospital where my father was slowly dy-ing. Fun story already, huh? Don't worry, it gets funnier in a bit. Stay with me.

One night, I found myself all alone in the big, empty house I had grown up in. God, what a sucky time. This Thanksgiving it was hard for me to feel thankful at all. It was hard to feel anything. I just wanted to escape.

I called my brother. "Eric, do you have any pot? I just wanna, like, zone out for a bit."

He got it. He was under the same stress I was. "Sorry. I don't have any weed, bro. But I have some pot butter in the freezer that'll do the trick. I could bring that over."

Pot butter? The idea of getting high by simply snacking on something scrumptious sounded exactly like the perfect cure for the moment, even if it was in the form of fattening butter. This was no time to think of my waistline; I just wanted to get wasted. "How soon can you be here?"

God bless my brother. About ten minutes later he came bursting through the front door. Before I knew it, he had sliced off a Paula Deen–sized portion of the pot butter, melted it in the microwave, and poured it over a piece of toast. "Eat this and you'll feel great in about twenty minutes."

Eventually, my brother left, informing me on his way out that he had put the remaining pot butter in the fridge in case I wanted any more. Trust me, I didn't want any more. In about three minutes, I was tripping my ever-lovin' nards off. I'd never been high like this before. It was fun, but scary, but fun. But scary. So I did what I always do when I'm scared: I called one of my best friends, Lisa.

Lisa still lived in our hometown and came over right away. By the time she arrived, I had calmed myself down and was in a warm and fuzzy place. Seeing how blissfully high I was, she immediately wanted in on the action. "Fire up the toaster, I want some of that!"

I did exactly as I had seen my brother do and made Lisa a delicious slice of pot-buttered bread. She made a face when she took the first bite. "Ugh! It tastes like a skunk wiped its butt on this."

In no time at all, we were laughing and smiling so much, our faces hurt. At one point, we laughed so hard that we began coughing, and I had to leave the room to get us both some water. When I returned just a few moments later, I found Lisa staring straight ahead with eyes like those creepy dolls that blink. She was as quiet as a stoned little mouse and she had two fingers on her neck, checking her pulse.

Still smiling, but confused, I asked, "Are you okay, honey bunny?"

She responded in the most serious tone I'd ever heard from anyone in my entire life. "I think my heart's going to explode."

"Oh, sweetie. Stop it," I said, trying to calm her. "Your heart is not going to explode."

"Ross, you don't understand." She was insistent, fanning herself with her hands to keep from crying. "While you were in the kitchen getting water, I was looking at a magazine and I swear to God, everyone in the magazine was looking back at me and now I'm freaking out. I'm not an expert or anything, but the pot butter must have mixed with my birth control or something and, I'm telling you, it's going to make my heart explode. I need you to call an ambulance."

I tried to reason with her. "Lisa, you're not even making sense! I am not calling an ambulance."

She got right in my face. "Ross, I'm not fucking around. I'm asking you as a friend. Please call a motherfucking ambulance!"

I should've just wrapped her up in a blanket and sang a soothing Enya song, but she had just used the F word twice in ten seconds. She'd never done that before, and it chilled me to the bone. Against my better judgment, I dialed 911.

"Nine-one-one, what's your emergency?" The operator was already freaking me out.

"Um, I'm visiting from college and have been super-stressed out, so my best friend and I did some pot to relax. It was very *The Big Chill*, you know? And now we're kinda, I don't know... her heart might be exploding? So can we get, like, an ambulance or whatever? And is it possible to request that they don't turn on their sirens, 'cuz I mean it's like ten o'clock at night and I don't want to bother my neighbors, you know?"

"Ma'am," the 911 operator told me flatly, "that's up to the driver's discretion."

Maybe it's because I was stoned out of my mind, but I swear before I even hung up the phone, I could hear an ambulance barreling into the driveway with sirens wailing like a dying Tyrannosaurus rex. The next thing I knew, we were in the back of the ambulance, still parked in front of my parents' house. I was kind of relieved. At least now there were medical professionals attending to Lisa, and things had settled down a bit. Then suddenly, out of nowhere, Lisa sat up and declared, "Oh my God, this is what it's like to die."

We all looked at her, and then at each other. She continued, "Yes, I get it now. Oh. My. God."

Holy shit, she was really beginning to lose it. Her delusional epiphany was building momentum at an alarming rate. "Oh dear God, I'm dying. Tell my parents I love them. Everything makes so much sense now. I never really thought *Seinfeld* was funny before, but now I get it. *I fucking get it! I fucking get Seinfeld!*"

Up to that point, I thought maybe calling an ambulance was overreacting. At that moment, I realized perhaps I'd made the right call.

As the ambulance pulled away with Lisa strapped in the back and me buckled in the front passenger seat, I turned to the driver and asked, "Is Lisa gonna die?"

"No," he responded sweetly. "She'll be just fine."

"Oh good." I was glad Lisa was going to live. "Am I going to die?"

"No, you're not dying, either."

Everything was spinning, my heart was beating overtime, and I was beginning to sweat profusely. "Are you sure? Because I really feel like I might be dying. My heart is beating super-hard."

The driver, keeping his eyes on the road and his left hand on the steering wheel, grabbed my wrist with his right hand and checked my pulse.

"Ted," he yelled to the medic tending to Lisa, "we've got another one!"

They rushed a mumbling Lisa and me into the emergency room in matching wheelchairs and booked us into a shared room. It was like a trauma slumber party. They gave us both something to calm us down and hooked us up to IVs filled with fluids. A nurse came in and asked me to sign something. I was confused. "Is this for my insurance?"

"No, it's for me," the nurse shamelessly replied. "Can you make it out to Nancy? I love you on *Leno*!"

Are you fucking kidding me? But I signed it anyway. Sometimes I'm just too nice.

Eventually, after Lisa had thrown up all over her hospital gown and I had eaten three servings of butterscotch pudding from the cafeteria, the doctor came into our room. "Okay, guys," he said in a patronizing tone, checking his clipboard, "you'll feel better soon."

I could feel his judgment. How dare he? I mean, we were good kids. We had just made a stupid mistake. I spoke up.

"You know what, Doctor? We're good kids. We just made a stupid mistake."

He paused at the door and looked back at us, over his glasses and down his nose like a cliché doctor character from a lame after-school special. "Yes, and that's why we don't do drugs."

As he left the room, Lisa and I looked at each other with shame, but then slowly began to chuckle. Even then, hooked up to EKGs and IVs, we just couldn't help ourselves.

We took a cab home and slept about ten hours that night. In the morning, Lisa and I could barely face each other, the humiliation hanging in the air as thick as the scent of vomit wafting from her hair. Like soldiers who had survived battle together, we now shared an unspoken bond that was even stronger than before. There was nothing more to say. We just hugged (I held my breath).

I knew I had to come clean when my mom finally got home from spending the night at the hospital in Seattle with my father. I knew if my mother forgave me, I could forgive myself. That's what parents do for us, right? I spent most of the day looking out the living room window for her blue Chevy Malibu to round the corner. When she finally arrived, I greeted her at the front door, ready to unload my tawdry tale of tainted toast.

She uncharacteristically slammed the door behind her. "I'm done!" she screamed, clearly exhausted and at her breaking point. "I am so sick and tired of it all. If I hear one more thing about a fucking hospital, I swear, I'm gonna punch someone in the goddamn face!"

I discreetly covered the hospital bracelet I'd purposely

kept around my wrist in hopes of enhancing the story that I'd so looked forward to telling her. As she stormed through the house swearing like a sailor, I thought to myself, *Well, I guess it can wait. She can just read all about it in my book one day.*

Chapter Thirteen

THE KWAN AND ONLY

As proud as I am of the person I've become, I also must acknowledge that I'm a complete and total failure. Sure, I've managed to cross off a few amazing items from my bucket list, but there is one item that, barring a small miracle or a major change in the rules for the Winter Olympic Games, shall forever remain on that list, glaring at me in all its annoyingly unfulfilled glory.

I'm like those Nerds candies that were my absolute favorite when I was a kid. The best flavor of Nerds were the ones that were Green Apple on the outside, but slowly dissolved in your mouth to reveal a hidden coating of Sour Red Cherry flavor on the inside. Sure, my personal outer coating may appear to be that of a well-rounded ball of happy-go-plucky positivity, but if you took the time to really delve deep into my psyche, you'd discover that inside me lives a tortured and embittered should-have-been Gold Medal–winning figure skater.

Wow! Total shocker, right? The gay guy loves figure skating! Whodathunk? Pick your jaw up from the floor and deal with it.

Figure skating! There is absolutely nothing more graceful than someone seemingly floating across the ice, alternating between flying through the air and spinning over and over and over again without vomiting on themselves. It's the perfect balance of athleticism and artistry.

I used to daydream about skating like that. And, oh, how my daydreams felt so real. I could almost feel it—the wind whipping my impossibly shiny hair as I spun through the air, the crowd leaping to their feet as I safely landed on mine. My purple-cotton-poly-blend pantsuit with matching chiffon cape, although flatteringly formfitting, would allow me full range of motion to express my innermost emotions on the ice. And, oh, how I would! The dazzled crowd would be on the edges of their seats and on the verge of tears as I dramatically ripped off my cape at the climactic crescendo of my signature performance music—the *Dawson's Creek* theme song, of course.

Yes, I always felt *certain* that I had that virtuoso skating ability living within me, just waiting to pop out like confetti or that scary baby monster thing in *Alien*. So when I finally did try figure skating for the first time, I was convinced that I would step onto the ice and instinctively glide effortlessly around the rink. I mean, sure it would take a few minutes before my first triple toe loop—that was understandable—but I knew without a doubt I'd finish my first lesson with a perfectly executed death spiral.

Well, it didn't exactly turn out like that. I never achieved a perfect death spiral during that first lesson, but I did very nearly spiral to my death. Instead of exploding onto the figure skating scene like some sort of red hot ingénue, I remained frozen in my skates, my legs wobbling like Bambi in that scene when he first learned to walk. It became suddenly clear that ice skating involved much more than just smiles, spandex, and sequins. It also took sweat, strength, and surprisingly sturdy ankles. Sadly, I had none of the above. I spent most of my first lesson facedown on the ice and faced with some cold, hard facts.

Although black and blue after my one and only attempt at figure skating, what hurt the most was the knowledge that as much as my mind could envision it, my body just wouldn't allow my inner gift to flourish. I felt like a marionette with severed strings, or one of those delusional people on *American Idol* who think they can sing but obviously can't. As frustrated as I was then, however, my love for the sport has never wavered and I have come to terms with—and even learned to love—my role as a mere spectator.

I don't want to brag or anything, but I was into figure skating way before it was cool. You know, before the entire world became interested in the sport during the gory glory days of the Tanya Harding and Nancy Kerrigan tragedy. What a wonderful game changer that was! Sure, Nancy's knee and Tonya's freedom were both sacrificed, but it was a magical time that finally brought figure skating into the mainstream. The whole thing was like a soap opera on skates. The crime! The video footage! The "will they or won't they compete on the ice" cliffhangers! And, the best of all, the so-bad-they're-good made-for-TV movies that followed! For a gay kid with a love of both figure skating and drama, it was almost too much.

In case you're an idiot who didn't follow every second of the excitement back then, or you're too young and haven't done your homework (kids these days...), let me fill you in on what went down: In order to secure Tonya Harding a spot on the US Olympic team, her husband, Jeff Gillooly, hired a big, scary guy to whack Tonya's biggest competition, Nancy Kerrigan, on the knee with a lead pipe ("WHY ME?!?!?"). I know it sounds like a game of Clue, but it really happened. What followed was a media shit storm the likes of which had never been seen before. This was pre–O. J. Simpson, pre–Michael Jackson molestation trial, pre–cat playing the piano on YouTube. It was *huge*. It was all anybody was talking about. It was nasty and tasteless. And, in my teenaged opinion, it was the most exciting thing that had ever happened. I was glued to the coverage 24/7.

All of this brouhaha built up to the day Nancy and Tonya finally skated at the 1994 Winter Olympics in Lillehammer, Norway, making an already thrilling event downright electrifying. I remember it like it was yesterday. Even though it was happening like nine time zones away, I was a nervous wreck. I remember frantically watching the clock in my seventh-grade Language Arts class and biting my nails, knowing that it was all happening right at that very moment. Lacking both logic and even one single ounce of human decency, my teacher wouldn't allow us to skip that day's chapter of *To Kill a Mockingbird*, even though I'd politely pointed out about fourteen times how easy it would be for us to just roll in the TV and watch, oh, I don't know, actual *his-*

tory in the making?!? I mean, I'm sorry, but classic literature will always be here. Harding vs. Kerrigan only happened that day. Get your priorities straight, lady.

It may shock you to learn that I was solidly in Tonya's corner. Yes, she was obviously guilty of orchestrating a violent attack on her biggest competitor and—almost as bad—had the most horrendous hair I'd ever seen, but I preferred her for two reasons. One, I like a little "trashy" in my women. Honey, a few bad highlights, permed bangs, and French-tipped acrylic nails never hurt anyone.

And two, Nancy had done something I could never forgive. Here's a little figure skating history lesson, dear reader: It was the 1994 US National Figure Skating Championships—six months prior to the Olympics—and Tonya Harding took first place. Nancy Kerrigan couldn't compete that night because she was still healing from her unfortunate knee injury. Sure, they were the most talked-about women in the world at that time, but for me, they were overshadowed that night. I remember watching it in my parents' living room, a bowl of Triscuits with a side of onion dip next to me, when I saw *her*. She may have been only thirteen years old and weighed about as much as the onion dip I'd devoured that night, but she took my breath away. Her name was Michelle Kwan, and she was undeniably the best figure skater I had ever seen. She soared with a weightless and effortless fluidity, like a sweet, romantic, otherworldly poem on the ice. I instantly became a faithful Kwanatonian and from that moment on have been loyal to my Kwan and Only.

Michelle Kwan's performance was perfect. The kind of

perfect you usually only experience listening to Justin Timberlake's first solo album or ordering the all-you-can-eat soup-and-salad special at Olive Garden. But even though she took second place that night at the US Championships, the Olympic Committee decided to *instead* take pity on Nancy Kerrigan and send *her* to the Olympics, cruelly discarding my beloved Michelle. So, even though Michelle had rightfully earned a spot in the 1994 games, she never even got her chance to compete! In the words of *Full House*'s Stephanie Tanner, "How rude!"

And that—that *right* there—is why I chose to root for Tonya, a knee-bashing hillbilly nincompoop, over Classy Nancy. Sure, it wasn't Nancy's fault that my precious Michelle was thrown under the Zamboni, but I had to take it out on someone.

Anyway, my love for both Nancy and Tonya was on thin ice after I fell under the spell of the Kwan. Going forward, there was nothing that would get in my way of watching Michelle skate. I didn't care if there were floods, famine, or a 50-percent-off sale—if she was on the ice skating, I was on the couch watching. That was why I freaked out so hard-core when, in my very early days as a correspondent on *The Tonight Show*, I got the assignment of a lifetime: covering the 2002 Winter Olympic Games in Salt Lake City. Holy shitballs, you guys. Do you know what this meant? I was going to be in the same city as the Kwan at the exact moment that she would, undoubtedly, win her first Olympic gold medal.

OMG. I had to meet her. Or, at the very least, if I couldn't meet her, I had to use the time I had on-air on NBC to make sure that Michelle Kwan knew, without a shadow of a doubt, that I was her biggest fan on the face of the planet.

And that's exactly what I did. Throughout the entire Winter Olympic Games, with every segment I shot and every live toss back to Jay Leno in the studio in Burbank, I would try to include an on-air message to my Michelle. Mind you, it was nothing supercreepy. Just something subtle like, "Oh, one more thing, Jay. I just want to say a big *hello* to the best figure skater in the entire world, Michelle Kwan. We're in the same city, honey—let's hang out!"

I kept waiting for the bigwigs at NBC to tell me to cut it out, but they never did. I think they thought my pathetic pseudostalker pleas were funny. I think they hoped, too, that perhaps Michelle would actually reach out in return and we could shoot an amazing segment where she and I actually met for the first time on air. Now *that* would be good television!

The highlight of my experience during the 2002 Winter Olympics in Salt Lake City was also the low point. One of my *Tonight Show* producers surprised me on the day of the women's figure skating long program competition with tickets to the big event. This was huge! Bigger than huge! This was the event where my Michelle would surely win her long-deserved gold medal, finally taking her rightful place among the ranks of the world's best skaters. A monumental moment for her, certainly, but even bigger for me. It felt like Christmas plus birthday plus the last day of school multiplied by a bazillion.

On the day of the competition, I couldn't even eat—*that* was how nervous I was to see her perform. I walked into the auditorium and immediately felt the energy. This was the Olympics. This mattered. The eyes of the world were focused on what was about to happen, and I was there to witness it all firsthand. As I took my seat and waited impatiently for the competition to start, the enormity and magnitude of the event hit me. How lucky was I? I knew for certain I'd tell my grandkids about this moment one day. Can't you just picture it? I'd be in my rocking chair, wrapped in a cashmere shawl while sipping Ensure out of a wineglass. "Chillun, come gather 'round Pop Pop," I'd mumble through my dentures and a Werther's Original butterscotch candy. "I'm gonna tell you young-uns 'bout the legend of the Kwan and how I was there to see her golden moment..."

As the event began and the other skaters took their turns, I wasn't worried. Call me biased, but this was no contest for the Kwan. I almost took a bathroom break when the USA's Sarah Hughes took the ice. I mean, she was good and all, but she wasn't even expected to medal. Even so, I decided to stay and support the home team.

That fucking Sarah Hughes. She was magical. She came out of nowhere and gave me chills, landing triple after triple after triple like some sort of beautiful figure skating phenom. As much as I hated to admit it, it was clear that this was a Kwan-caliber performance. The crowd was abuzz with shock and joy, counting the seconds down to the end of her program so they could erupt in applause and shower the ice rink below with roses and teddy bears. That fucking Sarah Hughes.

As magnificent as Sarah was, I wasn't panicking.

Michelle had this. All she had to do was not fall. That's it—just give the ol' Kwan razzle-dazzle, land her jumps, and she'd skate easily to the top of the medal podium.

To the roar of the crowd, Ms. Kwan stepped onto the rink looking even more radiant than usual. Her stunning crimson costume with gold detail was perfectly accented with her signature necklace, a Chinese good-luck charm her grandmother Yung Chun gave to her when she was just a ten-year-old girl (she never takes it off—look it up). The cheering audience went silent as Michelle took her place at the center of the ice.

As a selection from *Scheherazade*, the Russian symphonic suite by Nikolai Rimsky-Korsakov, began to echo throughout the arena, Michelle began her program, gliding toward her first series of jumps. I held my breath as she launched herself into the air. *Boom!* She landed it! *Thank God.* I exhaled and wiped my sweaty palms on my jeans. I felt like one of those fantastically annoying stage moms who coach their daughter's choreography from the audience at beauty pageants (God, I can't wait to have a daughter).

Then it was time for more jumps. *Boom!* Landed them again! That's my girl! As she rounded the far end of the rink and entered the last minutes of her performance, a wave of excitement replaced my nervousness as I realized she was actually going to do this. Just two more jumps and the gold was hers!

Boom. That was when it happened.

To be honest, dear reader, if it was up to me, I'd just end the chapter right here. It's just too painful for me to continue. I mean, I had to actually live through the experience once, and now you want me to relive it through the written word? How dare you? That's asking a lot of a man. But ever a champion, Michelle would want me to rise above my own great pain to tell the tale of her Great Fall. And so I shall.

Yeah, she fell. And it wasn't pretty. I suggest you look this performance up on YouTube, which I occasionally do when I'm in the mood to pair a nice Chardonnay with a freshly reopened wound. As you watch that fateful moment, listen closely and—I swear to Kwan—you can hear my horrified shriek piercing the otherwise muted gasps of the stunned crowd.

Michelle, of course, handled the fall gracefully and finished her routine like a consummate professional. I, on the other hand, completely lost my shit. The ramifications of this fall were huge. Insult to injury, the following and final skater (the aptly named Irina SLUTskaya) executed a nearly flawless performance, simultaneously securing Sarah Hughes's gold medal win, and knocking poor Michelle down to third. Bronze? *Bronze?* Do you know how hard it is to coordinate an outfit with *bronze*? This was shocking. This was soul-crushing. This was hands-down the worst thing that had happened to me since Shannen Doherty left *Beverly Hills 90210.*

For the remainder of the Olympics, I was completely inconsolable. My crew tried in vain to cheer me up. The last night of the games was the worst. Not only had I not met Michelle, but her dreams of Olympic gold had been crushed.

To mark the end of the Olympics, the *Tonight Show* crew had a celebratory dinner at the fanciest restaurant in all of Salt Lake City. I halfheartedly mustered up the will to put together an outfit for the occasion: black from head to toe—I was, after all, in mourning. Not even a gallon of Diet Coke and an entire basket of bread could pull me out of my funk. My chicken parmesan tasted a little saltier than I would've liked, undoubtedly because it was seasoned with my tears.

Toward the end of the meal, our waiter approached the table, no doubt to tell us about the dessert selection. Thank God. I couldn't wait to emotionally munch the bejeezus out of a piece of carrot cake. Instead, however, he leaned down to me and whispered, "Mr. Mathews, there's someone in the back who would love to meet you."

Oh, that's nice, I thought. *I guess one of those cute busboys recognizes me from TV.*

I followed the waiter through the kitchen, down a maze of long hallways, and through the double doors of what appeared to be an enormous private party in a fancy, exclusive dining room.

Before I could process what was happening, all eyes turned to me, and the large crowd rose from their tables and burst into thunderous applause. In a total stupor, I looked around the room and began clapping along with everyone else, having no clue what was going on. Little by little, it dawned on me that *I* was the reason everyone was clapping. The moment that realization sank in, the crowd parted and I saw *her.* As if in slow motion, she walked toward me, her ponytail swaying from side to side. She was carrying a single rose. It was Michelle Kwan.

"I hear you've been looking for me," she said with a humongous smile. She handed me the rose. "This is for you, Ross."

Holy fucking shit. Was this actually happening? Was I dreaming?

I took the rose. "Hi, I'm Ross."

Laughing, she replied, "I know, I heard you were here and I had to say hi. Thank you so much for all your support."

Then she hugged me, and as quickly as that magical moment began, it was over. I was whisked back to my table, back to the real world, and the next day back home to Los Angeles, clutching my rose the entire flight.

Who needs a stinkin' gold medal, anyway? Sure, my Michelle never won the Olympics. Big whoop. To me, she'll always be number one. I wouldn't give up the memory of that night—or the rose—for all the gold medals in the world. Most importantly, Michelle taught me a valuable lesson: Winning isn't everything. That is, of course, unless you're my future daughter and you're competing in a beauty pageant. Honey, don't embarrass Daddy. Second Place is First Loser. I'll settle for nothing less than Grand Supreme, and I'm not talking about a Taco Bell burrito.

Chapter Fourteen

THE MOST WONDERFUL TIME OF THE YEAR

I think you guys know by now that I would never ever say anything bad about anyone, but if you're not totally 100 percent into the undeniable magic, wonder, and goodwill of the holiday season like I am, then, frankly, you should probably rot in hell. And if you don't like it, you can just suck my candy cane.

Damn right, I'm holly jolly. I'm straight up Ho-Jo. I'm Ho-Jo like a Mo-Fo. I'm a Ho-Jo Mo-Fo Homo! Watch out—I could do this all night!

It really roasts my chestnuts how some people get depressed around the holidays. I've got so much Christmas cheer, I feel it's my duty to pay it forward. In fact, I'm thinking of starting a hotline that bummed-out bah-humbugs and gloomy Grinches can call to get a heapin' helpin of holiday happiness.

A recording of my angelic voice would pull them from the depths of their December despair. "Ho Ho Ho, this is Ross! Thanks for calling! Press 1 if you're experiencing seasonal depression. Press 2 if your family is driving you crazy. Press 3 if you're freaking out because you just ate a six-pound box of See's Candies while watching Melissa Joan Hart in a very special ABC Family Christmas Movie about a homeless girl with a heart of gold who discovers that the Santa in the mall is her real father."

I would watch the hell out of that movie, by the way.

I'm telling you, I love the holidays so much that if I were in charge of things, they would be celebrated all year long. You could totally observe Christmas, or Hanukkah, or Kwanzaa, or whatever jingles your bell.

I just adore the holiday season. Why? Because giving gifts makes me happy, receiving gifts makes me even happier, and good old-fashioned stick-to-your-ribs kinda holiday home cookin' makes me the hap-hap-happiest of all!

That's why I start celebrating Christmas at 12:01 a.m. the morning after Halloween. Sure, there's still Thanksgiving to get through, but let's be honest—that's kind of a faux holiday. Where are the gifts? Where are the twinkle lights? Where are the shiny decorations? I'm sorry, but a cut-out construction paper handmade into a turkey does not a centerpiece make. It just ain't gonna cut it.

Sure, Thanksgiving food is yummy. I always spend Thanksgiving in Los Angeles and celebrate the traditional way—you know, with a turkey. The only difference is that in California, we get a free-range fair-trade fat-free turkey that was raised on an organic farm and fed the Zone Diet by biracial yoga-instructing Wiccan lesbians. Delish!

However, my favorite Thanksgiving food-related tradition is absolutely sinful. Every year I make my favorite dish in the history of the entire world, my Nana's Famous Potatoes. Nana was my great-grandma, and believe you me, the woman knew her way around a potato. She could really take a spud for a spin! I swore on a stack of pecan pancakes that I'd never divulge the supersecret family recipe, but like the plot twist in *Citizen Kane*, the plot twist in *The Crying Game*, and the plot twist in *The Sixth Sense*, it's a secret that I just can't seem to keep (Rosebud's a sled, she's a he, and Bruce Willis is dead. Oops, I did it again!).

Nana's Famous Potatoes dish is a great go-to meal that you can bust out when you want to impress your friends and family. They're gonna love it! It's an irresistible cheesy, potatoey, Corn Flake-y dream come true. They're beyond addictive. If I ever end up "guest-starring" on *Intervention*, it'll be because I found a way to mainline Nana's delicious taters straight into my bloodstream. I mean, it's not like I have a real problem, man. I could quit it anytime I want, I just don't wanna. And once you try 'em, neither will you.

So here, available to the public for the very first time ever, is the top-secret recipe for my Nana's Famous Potatoes on the actual recipe card my mom sent me when I wanted to make it for my friends in 2002 at my first grown-up Easter (another worthwhile holiday):

Recipe: Nana's O'Brien Potatoes
From: Mom   Makes: a lot

32 oz. package frozen hash browns
Break! up into 9x13 pan. Mix 2 c.
sour cream with 2 c. grated
cheese. Spread over potatoes.

Mix ½ c. melted margarine with
1 cup Corn Flakes. Put on top.

Bake 325° 1 or 1½ hrs. (over)

©CURRENT, INC., COLORADO SPRINGS, CO 80941

It's good hot, it's good cold, and it's even better on the second day. Normally, this recipe serves eight to ten people, but if you're going through a particularly bad break-up, it just serves one. Enjoy!

So, yes, Nana's Famous Potatoes are a Thanksgiving highlight. But as undeniably good as the food is during Thanksgiving, you know as well as I do that, bless its well-meaning little heart, Thanksgiving is just an opening act, a pit stop on the way to the main event on December 25.

It may sound harsh, but Thanksgiving shmankshmiving. I mean, for a holiday with the word *giving* right in its name, there really isn't a lot of giving going on at all. Unless, of course, you count *giving* yourself heartburn by eating one too many helpings of Aunt Marjorie's greasy green bean casserole or *giving* your cousin Barry the stink-eye for eating the last of the pumpkin pie before you got to taste any.

Worse yet? Unlike Christmas, Thanksgiving doesn't even have *one* traditional song. I dare you to name a single example off the top of your head. Mmm-hmm, I didn't think so, Pilgrim.

I rest my case. Christmastime is awesome, no matter what you celebrate. That's why, if I had only three wishes, along with world peace and a *Friends* reunion (not necessarily in that order), I would decree that all citizens of Earth celebrate the holidays every single day of the year.

Now, I know all you Scrooges are scrunching up your noses and scoffing, "Christmas year-round? Ho Ho *No!* That would get *really* old *really* quick. Fa-la-la-lame!"

Well, I've got as many arguments in favor of my mandatory Year-Round Yuletide as I have twinkle lights on my tree. So, get ready for your snow globe to be shaken *and* stirred, 'cuz I'm about to stuff your stocking with some festive facts!

First, until recently, the holidays were the only time of the year when Starbucks offered their famously addictive sugar-free peppermint syrup. Now, I don't know about you, but I go frappin' crazy for a holiday drink. I used to get so angry every January when my barista would break the news to me, "So sorry, Ross. We don't have sugar-free peppermint anymore. As I told you last year...and the year before...we only have it during the holidays."

What a joke! I was irate. I wanted to personally punch the party pooper who prevented the public from perpetually purchasing pumps of peppermint! Why shouldn't I be able to guzzle a guilt-free drink of my choice 365 days a year? But, luckily for us all, Starbucks saw the "lite," and it now offers not only sugar-free peppermint, but many other holiday-inspired sugar-free syrups year round (including vanilla, hazelnut, and cinnamon dolce). God bless Starbucks for their sugar-free, calorie-free syrups. Seriously, they should get the Nobel Treats Prize for inventing those.

Secondly, Christmas has the very best holiday mascot of them all. Yep, it's undeniable that Santa Claus towers over all the others, both figuratively and literally. I mean, who's his competition: an Easter Bunny, the St. Paddy's Day leprechaun, Cupid, and a freakin' *groundhog*? Puh-lease. Sure, Santa may be pushing about four hundred pounds, but he could run laps around those lazy bums!

Think about it! Santa has given us bikes, dollhouses, train sets, and Cabbage Patch Kids. The least we could do is return the favor and give him a little more respect. I mean, seriously, after all these years, he still just has a part-time job?!? Imagine the joy he could bring to girls and boys on a daily basis. The cookie-and-milk industry would benefit as well!

But, truthfully, the main reason I'm such a sucker for celebrating this particular season is that it brings back so many wonderful memories. Growing up in the Mathews family, Christmas wasn't necessarily about the meaning of giving or celebrating baby Jesus' birthday. Instead, Christmas was an excuse for my parents to get festively shit-faced with their friends, neighbors, and coworkers while my brother and I watched in sheer horror.

Absolutely everyone who was anyone in my small town made a point to stop by our open house for Christmas Eve. Why? Because my dad knew how to party. He'd put on his one and only red sweater, splash on enough Brut aftershave to drown an elf, and put away about a half a bottle of generic-brand whiskey before Mom had even put out the Lit'l Smokies and nut-covered cheese ball.

He'd have a nice buzz going on by the time people started showing up, and in an effort to really kick the party up a notch, he would put on his favorite cheesy Christmas music, sung by a Scandinavian artist named Stan Boreson ("Oh, I yust go nuts at Christmas, da best time of da year…").

I remember being absolutely mortified when my English teacher (and my mom's best friend) would, for one night, set aside her painstakingly precise enunciation and begin slurring and swearing like a sloshed sailor. And I remember hiding in shame when my dad's friends from the school board all knocked back shot after shot of vodka chased with a hot buttered rum and began to arm-wrestle.

Yes, I was utterly mortified back then. But what I didn't understand is that Christmas parties are like a weekend in Las Vegas—what happens there stays there. And now, to be completely honest with you, my parents' holiday parties sound like they would've been a total freaking blast. It's been nearly a decade since my dad died, but I would give absolutely anything to experience the holidays as a grown-up with him. I picture us arm in arm and drunk as skunks as we sing Stan Boreson songs at the top of our lungs. Just thinking about it, I can almost smell his aftershave.

Perhaps the dream of creating my own holiday traditions is why I'm so adamant about making a big deal of celebrating the holidays. Year after year, I find myself more and more insistent on starting traditions and forcing all those around me to follow through. For example, it is essential that my friends gather at our house before December 1 each year to assist in putting up our Christmas tree. As we hang ornaments, string lights, and get drunk on hot toddies, we *will* listen to Mariah Carey's Christmas album on repeat whether they like it or not.

And I don't just have one tree. What do you think I am, some kind of beginner? No! I simply must have one tree in the living room and one tree in the back of the house. It's essential, not because I'm a fancy person who thinks he deserves two trees, but because I have some very, um, special ornaments that can't be displayed for everyone to see. Let me explain...

The year was 2002. It was my first Christmas since graduating college and my first Christmas in my very own apartment, a two-bedroom cockroach-infested shithole I shared with my best friend, Taya. Located in one of Los Angeles's less desirable neighborhoods, our apartment was on Normal Avenue. No joke. Normal Avenue. I can't make this shit up.

Taya and I were determined to make our first official grown-up Christmas an event to remember, even if our combined total income that month was less than what most people spend on toothpaste. Sure, we were flat broke, but our holiday spirit could not be broken.

In order to decorate appropriately, yet within our nonexistent budget, we had to get creative. Instead of buying an expensive Christmas tree, we ventured out onto the rough streets of East Los Angeles, found a green pinelike tree (quite a feat in LA), cut off a branch, brought it home, and stuck it in an old coffee can. Viola! Insta-tree.

Our real creativity came out when it was time for us to decorate the tree. Fancy store-bought ornaments were a luxury we simply could not afford, but neither one of us was going to let our tree be naked for the duration of the holidays. Not in our household!

The idea hit us while we were walking to the coffee shop. It was our routine to grab a free newspaper on our route and read it while we sipped our coffee. You know those weird newspapers with "scandalous personal ads" and advertisements for "massage therapists" in the back? The borderline pornographic ones with naked women and men looking all sensual and sexy and ready to do things that are illegal in every state but Nevada? Taya and I loved reading those.

It was while we were reading the ads and laughing that it

hit us both, almost simultaneously: we could use these sexy newspaper massage ads on our tree!

We grabbed a few more free newspapers and rushed home. Next, we found an old shoebox and cut out small ornament-sized circles and squares that we wrapped tightly in tinfoil. Finally, we cut out our favorite sensual massage ads and taped them to the tinfoil circles and squares, attached them to a string, and hung them on our tree.

We stepped back to admire our handiwork. It was a Christmas Miracle. The Miracle on Normal Avenue, you could say. Not only had we decorated our makeshift tree, we had done the unthinkable—we had created a new kind of holiday decoration. When we couldn't afford an ornament, we created the Pornament. Talk about a "happy ending."

And the real topper? We sacrificed an old *People* magazine, cut out a picture of Oprah—the Universe's brightest, most angelic star—and placed her at her rightful spot atop our tree. You may now feel free to applaud.

So you see, the holiday season, specifically Christmas, has always been a beautiful time for me—a time of family, food, and fun, no matter how much money we had. It's unlike any other time in the year. So humor me for a while, dear reader, and open your mind to the possibility of celebrating the holiday spirit 365 days a year. If you concentrate closely enough, you might just hear sugar plums dancing. You also might hear Suga' Plumm dancing—she was one of the exotic dancers on our Pornaments. God bless us, every one.

Chapter Fifteen

LIKE A PRAYER

I must admit something to you, dear reader: I've been a bad gay. No, I didn't eat at Chic-fil-A or go a full month without a pedicure. My God, nothing that serious. But I do have to make a confession. A *Confession on a Dance Floor*, if you will. What I'm about to tell you is "Borderline" unforgivable, but I must "Express Myself." Are you sitting down? Okay, here it is: I haven't always loved Madonna.

I know, I know, sacrilege! But, when it came to the Material Girl, it took me quite a while to get "Into the Groove." I mean, sure, I like a good beat and catchy chorus as much as any red-blooded American boy, but as a young child, I just couldn't get past her tacky over-accessorizing and shamelessly exposed midriff. She was a bad girl and I was a good boy. I'm sorry, Madonna, but back then, I just wasn't "Crazy for You."

In all honesty, I think she scared me. She was always crawling on the floor and rolling around with a seductive smile on her face. She looked like the type of person who had lots of sex with lots of different people. Quite frankly, I found it all a bit too much for my preteen pop culture palate. And Madonna's worst sin of all? Those god-awful eyebrows. Ugh. Unruly, out of control, and in your face, just like her.

They say there's a thin line between love and hate, and I quickly "Vogue'"'d right over that line when I suddenly went from being disgusted with Madonna to being delighted by her. The movie was *Who's That Girl?* and it had me asking the very same question. Sure, her eyebrows were worse than ever, but for some reason they kind of grew on me.

If it had been up to me, I wouldn't have even bothered seeing that movie at all. But fate intervened one night, and I was lured into my neighbor's basement by all my favorite snacks. I didn't care what tape my neighbor popped into the VHS player, as long as she popped some Orville Redenbacher's in the microwave while she was at it. Honestly, putting Madonna in a movie sounded to me like about as good an idea as chocolate-covered raisins (raisins are already nature's candy, stupid), but, just like Raisinettes, somehow *Who's That Girl?* worked.

Madonna played Nikki Finn, a sassy gum-popping trollop packed into a skintight dress, with white blonde hair and black caterpillar Groucho Marx eyebrows. With just one look, the uptight repulsion I had originally felt for the gap-toothed, crotch-grabbing chameleon was replaced by a downright obsession. I guess you could say I drank the Madonna Kool-Aid, and it was not just satisfyingly sweet, but terrifically tart.

From that moment forward, I was a full-fledged, card carrying Madonna minion. Wherever her cone-shaped boobies pointed, I followed. And what a journey we went on! From daring dominatrix, to disco diva, to demure darling, and every look in between, I've been a proud barnacle, steadfastly attached to the underside of the SS *Madonna* as it sailed to "La Isla Bonita" and beyond!

The planets aligned when I was a sophomore in high school. The year was 1996, the pinnacle of Madonna mania, when she hit us with the triple whammy of giving birth to a baby, an album, and a movie musical spectacular all at once! The child was named Lourdes. The album, *Ray of Light*. The film, *Evita*. What a year.

Ray of Light, with its global message of spirituality mixed with cross-continental beats, spoke to me like an album never had before. And *Evita*? Dear God, *Evita*. Broadway legend Andrew Lloyd Webber outdid himself with that one! But unlike the second L in Mr. Webber's middle name, Madonna's brilliance in that film could never be silenced. She gave a restrained, honest, and heartbreaking performance, commanding the type of respect from movie critics and audiences alike that had, up until that point, eluded her. And all those accolades were well deserved. I mean, sure, she was playing a blindly ambitious husband-stealing Nazi sympathizer, but her hair finally matched her eyebrows!

Can you keep a secret, Argentina? I did cry, not just for you, but also for Madonna when she was awarded a coveted Golden Globe for her stellar performance in *Evita*. Who would've thought that the same girl who, merely years before, was wearing those ridiculous golden, cone-shaped brassieres would one day be clutching a Golden Globe to her heaving bosom? It didn't take an awards show expert like myself to know that somebody on Madonna's household staff had better make room on her mantel for what would inevitably follow—a prize that would make her Golden Globe seem like it came from the bottom of a Cracker Jack box: an Oscar.

I awoke bright and early on the morning of that year's Oscar nominations. After all, people, this was history in the making. Like Cher before her, this year Madonna would undoubtedly join the ranks of one-named pop icons who were recognized by the Academy of Motion Picture Arts and Sciences. As I prepared my breakfast of strawberry Pop-Tarts slathered in peanut butter (my invention—peanut butter and jealous, much?), I rehearsed my reaction for when I would finally hear her name announced as a Best Actress nominee. My choices ran the gamut, ranging from a smugly satisfied smile to girlishly gleeful giddiness. It never even occurred to me to rehearse a reaction for the worst-case scenario.

Eventually, after the pesky supporting categories were announced, it was time for the main event: Best Actress. Previous Oscar winner Mira Sorvino and Academy president Arthur Hiller began, announcing the five nominees in the customary alphabetical order, "The nominees for Best Actress are... Brenda Blethyn for *Secrets and Lies*, Diane Keaton for *Marvin's Room*, Frances McDormand for *Fargo...*"

Huh? I thought to myself, confused. *Doesn't Madonna come before McDormand? Is it Mc-Dormand or Mac-Dormand?*

They continued. "...Kristin Scott Thomas for *The English Patient...*"

What was going on?!? I was beginning to lose my shit. There was only one name left, and unless in my excitement I had completely lost comprehension of the English alphabet, that name was not going to be the one I wanted to hear.

"...And, finally, Emily Watson for *Breaking the Waves*."

Surprise nominee Emily Watson broke more than just waves that morning; she also broke my spirit and, no doubt, Madonna's heart. I couldn't believe it. The unthinkable had happened. Madonna wasn't nominated. I woke up that day ready to "Celebrate," but here I was "True Blue."

I felt numb, then enraged, then concerned. I couldn't help but picture Madonna watching these nominations herself, buckling to her knees in heartache. I yearned to rush to her side to comfort her, hold her up and whisper in her ear, "Madonna, you were robbed! You didn't just *play* Evita, you *were* Evita! No one can take that away from you. Ever! Your performance was just too transcendent—it flew right over the Oscar voters' heads. You were *so* real, *so* seamless, they didn't even know it was acting! That's why you weren't nominated—you were too good!"

Instead, and because I didn't know Madonna's home address, I simply stayed home from school that day and polished off the entire box of Pop-Tarts, the rest of the jar of peanut butter, the leftover Salisbury steak from dinner the previous night, a canister of sour cream and onion Pringles, and a six-pack of sugar-free tapioca puddin' cups. If Madonna wasn't going to have to worry about fitting into a skintight, unforgiving couture gown for the Oscars, then neither would I. It was an act of solidarity.

Sometimes heartbreak can weaken a relationship, but it only strengthened ours. One would think that my admiration for her would have diminished throughout the years, but it—like her arms—only grew stronger. As the years ticked by, I've loved loving her from afar, never dreaming that one day I might possibly meet her. I mean, how would that even happen? After all, we live in completely different worlds. I'm over here in the real world, full of everyday annoyances like hangnails and flat tires, while she's off in a faraway soft-focus fantasy world inhabited by young, sinewy Latino backup dancers and delicious raw vegan snacks.

Let's be honest, the chance of our very different worlds ever colliding seemed unlikely, to say the least. It seems strange for me, the dreamer of all dreamers, to have been so uncharacteristically pessimistic about the possibility of meeting the one and only Madonna Louise Ciccone in the flesh. After all, I had somehow beaten the odds and managed to meet nearly all my other female idols, including goddesses like Tiffani-Amber Thiessen, Liza Minnelli, Michelle Kwan, Oprah, Rue McClanahan, and not one but two of Madonna's besties, Gwyneth Paltrow and Rosie O'Donnell. But for some reason, and this is not to in any way diminish the star wattage of the lovely ladies above, meeting Madonna seemed an impossible feat. I mean, if I allowed myself to dream of meeting Madonna, why not hope to meet fellow superstars on the same otherworldly level—stars such as Santa Claus, the Tooth Fairy, or Jared from Subway? Things like that just don't happen.

Oh ye of little faith. Despite everything you've just read, I think you know how this story ends. Yep, that's right, it ends with me not just meeting, but actually *touching* the most famous blonde on Planet Earth since Marilyn Monroe. Are you sitting? Because this one's a doozy...

Here's how it happened. When my *Tonight Show* writer, Anthony, and I found out that Madonna was performing at Dodger Stadium, just a stone's throw from the NBC Studios in Burbank, we suddenly had a crazy, harebrained idea. We rushed to our producers, hoping they'd love it as much as we did. Keep in mind, this was in October 2008, and I had already been a *Tonight Show* correspondent for nearly six years. By then I had done everything from skydiving and competing in a demolition derby to interviewing Sydney Poitier and Sarah Ferguson, the Duchess of York. We were always looking for a fresh, new idea. This one was not only fresh and new, but relatively simple: I, an out-of-control Madonna fan, would do whatever it took to sneak backstage and meet the star herself.

Just as we had hoped, the producers loved it, but added one more challenging twist. Meeting her wasn't enough—I had to also make physical contact with Madonna. My mission, should I choose to accept it, was to touch one of the most untouchable people in show business. Of course, all of this was to be filmed and aired on national television. No pressure, right?

WARNING: *Baby's got a Secret.* I am now going to lift the curtain and expose a rarely admitted show business practice. I feel like one of those jerks who ruins the magic trick for everyone, but I truly believe that it's important to share the truth with you all. If Operation Touch Madonna failed, not only would it turn out to be a major bummer, but it would also be a total waste of time and money. If I didn't succeed, we couldn't even air it.

The problem? It's never a good idea to surprise someone who employs more people on her security team than the population of many small countries. It would not only end in disappointment, but with one's face—I'm going to guess mine—smooshed against the cold, dirty concrete floor of Dodger Stadium. I mean, I wanted this to happen, but I also wanted to "Live to Tell."

So we had our people contact Madonna's people and run the idea by her. And to both her credit and my amazement, she agreed. Sure, I was thrilled to know that I wouldn't be tackled by one of her enormous bodyguards as I approached the pop star backstage, but I was even more thrilled to finally be meeting her. Somehow, though, I still couldn't believe it. I hadn't been this thrown for a loop since that horrifying Oscar travesty so many years earlier.

I didn't tell a single soul about the plan, so as not to jinx it. No one knew: not my mother, my roommate, or even my Starbucks barista—people who were usually kept abreast and in the mix when it came to my comings and goings.

Even on the day of the concert, I didn't believe it would really happen. Even after I buckled my seatbelt in the NBC van, and then pulled into the stadium parking lot and was escorted through the VIP security check-in backstage, I still somehow couldn't accept the reality of what was going on. I think I had residual emotional pain from Madonna's Oscar snub. I mean, I had believed wholeheartedly in that certainty, too, but it didn't happen. I just couldn't go through that again.

Looking around Dodger Stadium, it dawned on me that I had been to a few games there many years ago. I guess you could say "This Used to Be My Playground." But I was on Madonna's turf now and nervous that my dream might be shattered even before it began.

However, I knew without a doubt that I had penetrated the inner circle when I saw Madonna's longtime infamous publicist, Liz Rosenberg, approaching me. Everyone knows that it was easier to get a seat on a *Titanic* lifeboat than it is to get within one hundred yards of Madonna, but when Liz said, "Ross, it's so nice to meet you," it was suddenly clear that this was, in fact, real. I knew then and there that this was going to be a day I would always "Cherish."

What happened next happened very quickly. It was like a blur, the details of which I remember as if they happened two seconds ago. I can recall every sound, every smell, every thought I had. Liz Rosenberg guided me into a large tent, a makeshift oasis in the Dodger Stadium parking lot. Inside, there were white flowers everywhere with matching white couches, carpets, and drapes in every corner. I'm actually pausing right now to really ponder...was that what it was really like? But I swear to God, dear reader, it was. Also, the temperature inside the tent was perfect. Not too chilly, not too warm. Just right. Was this heaven? I wasn't sure, but it certainly had heaven's color scheme.

I was snapped back to reality when Liz Rosenberg once again appeared out of nowhere and informed me, "Madonna will be out shortly—make yourself comfortable."

That was it? *Make yourself comfortable*? No *Sit there and don't touch a thing*?

I immediately started exploring. I felt like a kid at the circus as I watched gorgeous, young backup dancers stretching. Muscular roadies in Crew T-shirts hastily came and went like speeding cars whizzing past me. Slick security officers in Italian suits and mirrored sunglasses spoke in hushed tones over walkie-talkies. And then I saw two of the most exciting features of the Madonna Circus—the positively adorable fruits of her limber loins, Lourdes and Rocco. I shamelessly stared at them like exotic zoo animals, wondering what it must be like to be them and, more important, what it must be like to have a mother named Madonna. But like a pair of precocious pandas, they were completely clueless as to how many eyes were on them, and they simply ran around, playing a game of Tag.

Suddenly the temperature in the room got colder, or warmer—I couldn't really tell—and everybody turned around simultaneously to watch Madonna emerge from her dressing room and saunter down the stairs like a glamorous silent movie star. "Come on, everybody," Madonna said in her newly acquired British accent, "it's time for the prayer circle."

Oh my God, I thought. *The prayer circle?!? THE Prayer Circle?!?*

I'd seen *Truth or Dare*—Madonna's black-and-white concert documentary—about a gazillion times, and I knew what the prayer circle was. Before each concert, Madonna would gather the concert cast and crew—musicians, dancers, and backup singers alike—and lead them in a prayer. Everyone knows about Madonna's prayer circle, but hardly anyone's ever been in one. That's precisely why I didn't waste any time hopping into that circle, grabbing the hands of the two strangers on either side of me, and bowing my head faster than you can say, "Like a Prayer"!

We all closed our eyes as Madonna began the prayer: "Let's have a really good show, everyone. We've all worked very hard and the audience deserves our best..."

That's the moment I felt someone brush against me. I opened my eyes and saw a blonde woman in white walking behind the circle, making her way toward Madonna. *How rude,* I thought. *What kind of person—other than me, of course—barges into a private, preshow prayer circle? This is sacred, dammit.*

Finally, Madonna noticed the woman, as well, and I focused on the Queen of Pop's face, bracing for a stormy reaction to this tart's tacky trespassing. But instead of contempt, Madonna showed compassion. She stopped what she was saying, hugged the woman, invited her into the circle and continued, "Everyone, make room for Britney."

Say what?

Madonna continued. "As you know, she's had a really hard time of late..."

Did she just say Britney?

"...what with the press and the paparazzi and all..."

Oh my God, it can't be.

"...She needs us now."

I finally let my eyes drift from Madonna's face to that of the mystery woman in white and there she was: everyone's favorite former Mouseketeer turned Pop Princess turned Justin Timberlake-ex, Britney Fuckin' Spears.

Britney's hair had grown out from her unfortunate headline-grabbing tango with an electric razor just enough to hold extensions. She looked surprisingly together and much less catatonic than one would expect. Seeing Britney in the circle, Madonna's hand generously radiating a maternal love and support right into hers, I could imagine Britney graduating from a 5150 on a psych ward chart to number one on the pop charts again. Just then, Madonna's reputation as a controlling taskmaster melted away, revealing a genuinely caring mentor and friend.

This was the fucking best moment of my life. This was magical on so many levels. It was simultaneously real and unreal. I was so caught up in the moment that I almost forgot my mission. Sure, Madonna had just touched my heart, but I still hadn't touched her.

The prayer circle had barely uttered "Amen" when Liz Rosenberg grabbed me and instructed, "Meet us at the back door in ten seconds."

I did as I was told and rushed over immediately. I didn't even have time to catch my breath before She was in front of me in all her majestic glory. The thing about Madonna up close, dear reader? She's perfect, just perfect. A "Beautiful Stranger," if you will. As my cameraman rolled, I told her that Jay Leno had sent me to not just meet her, but cop a feel as well. Without missing a beat, she regally extended her hand, as if to grant me permission to make physical contact. Knowing she was not going to leave her hand out for long, I instinctively made my move. I told her I loved her and touched her, "Like a Virgin," for the very first time.

In a heartbeat, she was gone. She may have had only "4 Minutes" to save the world, but she had just changed mine in less than four seconds.

I know this all sounds too good to be true, like one of those made up *Bedtime Stories*. But it all happened, I swear to Kabbalah. And you may think I'm crazy for caring so much, but I'm not sorry...

It's "Human Nature."

Chapter Sixteen

SQUASH INJUSTICE

At the risk of sounding too hippy-dippy, I believe we all have the power to change the world. I don't say this as a spectator, a mere cheerleader shaking his pompoms on the sidelines. No, I say it as a brave soldier on the battlefield in the war against gross injustices.

Indulge me for a minute, dear reader, while I fill you in on a little backstory. I've been blogging for years. I began my online obsession in 2006 while I was covering the Winter Olympic Games in Torino, Italy, for *The Tonight Show*. I started blogging as a way for my mother to follow my adventures, and once it gained a sizeable following, I just fell in love with it.

Blogging is a format like no other, a way of connecting with people from all over the world on a daily basis. I lovingly refer to those who frequent HelloRoss.com as "blog buddies" and delight in maintaining a familylike online community of fun folks.

A signature feature on my website is what I call Talky Blogs. They're basically video blogs on steroids. They consist of me in front of the camera just chattin' about life and whatnot. Not long after I created Talky Blogs, they really took off. I'd post one at night, and by the next morning, it would have, like, twenty thousand views. It blew my mind that I had that kind of far-reaching appeal.

As the years went by, my website continued to grow in popularity. This was the time in my life when I had just finished taping the reality show *Celebrity Fit Club*, where I transformed my body and lost over forty pounds by starving myself and competing against people like Screech and DaBrat in kayak races. I was trying to maintain my recent weight loss without the scrutiny of being weighed in on national television (talk about pressure). So when I found a meal option that was not only healthy but delicious, I latched onto it like Scooby Doo on a Scooby snack.

Koo-Koo-Roo is a fast food restaurant chain that sells amazingly flavorful rotisserie chicken and figure-friendly, heart-healthy side dishes. You may be thinking to yourself, *Koo-Koo-What?* but everybody in Los Angeles knows Koo-Koo-Roo. It's a very popular regional chain. Just ignore the fact that the name sounds like a delightfully crazy drag queen. "Ladies and gentlemen, please welcome to the stage...Cuckoo Ru!"

I'd frequent Koo-Koo-Roo about three days a week. I wouldn't say I was addicted, but I was definitely a recreational user. My dinner ritual was to order the brilliant trifecta of one succulent rotisserie-grilled chicken breast, a side of freshly steamed green beans, and—my favorite—a sizeable scoop of golden butternut squash. I fully understand that butternut squash is not a food that people are generally passionate about, but I don't even care. I *love* squash! I have since I was just a toddler. Sure, it has the consistency of baby food and the color of baby poop, but my taste buds just go goo-goo-ga-ga for it.

I'm a purist when it comes to my squash, and Koo-Koo-Roo did it just right—no salt, no pepper, no butter. Nothin' but sweet, scrumptious, straightforward squash, *au naturel*. You can't improve on perfection, am I right?

We had a good thing going on, Koo-Koo-Roo and I. Smooth sailin' all the way, you know what I mean? Little did I know that my restaurant love affair was about to be served up with a side order of major disappointment.

It was a beautiful evening, just like any other in Los Angeles. Per usual, I dropped by my local Koo-Koo-Roo for a good ol' breast, beans, 'n' butternut buffet. For some reason, though, the staff seemed a little more quiet than usual. Almost sad in a way? Something told me that the secret ingredient tonight would be an herb called OregaNO-You-Didn't!

As I approached the cash register, the manager stopped me before I even opened my mouth to place my regular order. I'd always loved this Koo-Koo-Roo manager lady. She was beautiful and looked exactly like Pocahontas from the animated Disney movie. And just like Pocahontas led John Smith through the dangerous wilderness of the new west, this Koo-Koo-Roo manager, whose name I can't seem to remember for the life of me (sorry, honey!), led me to some of the worst news I had ever received.

"Ross, I don't know how to tell you this. We don't have squash anymore."

I blinked, a little confused. "You mean you ran out?"

She took a deep breath and blew her blunt bangs from her forehead as if she was about to break into her rousing rendition of "Colors of the Wind." Instead, she took the wind out of my sails and the color out of my face. She frowned and said, "No, Ross. They discontinued it. It's not coming back."

Are...you...kidding me? My beloved butternut squash was no more? How could this be? I couldn't believe it. I asked her, "No squash?!? What am I supposed to order instead? Rice pilaf? Spinach? Broccoli?!? What kind of world are we living in?!?"

"I'm so sorry, Ross. We didn't even want to tell you," she explained sheepishly. "Have you tried our creamed corn?"

Seriously? Creamed corn? I'd always liked my Koo-Koo-Roo Pocahontas, but now she was really getting on my nerves. Replacing my beloved squash with creamed corn was like substituting fine champagne with a tacky strawberry daiquiri wine cooler. Thanks, but no thanks!

With a frown and much less sparkle than usual, I begrudgingly ordered my chicken breast and green beans, and sadly settled for a side of subpar, carbo-loaded mashed potatoes. Mashed potatoes? Who had I become? I could barely recognize myself anymore.

As Pocahontas handed me my receipt, she circled a toll-free 1-800 number and gave me a slight glimmer of hope. "If you really want to do something about it, you can call this number to express your concerns to our home office. You'll probably never hear back, but still, you should let them know."

Damn straight I would call! These Koo-Koo-Roo corporates had flown the coop, and I was determined to set them straight when it came to the pecking order of my favorite vegetables. Someone had to squash this kind of squash injustice!

So I hatched a plan to get my favorite chicken chain to listen. I walked to my car and called the toll-free number right away. I didn't even open up my dinner first—that was how important this was. The message I left on the Koo-Koo-Roo customer service voice mail was passionate and sincere, a moving plea for justice and the God-given right to indulge in the sweet satisfaction of butternut bliss.

Next, I turned on the compact camcorder I used to film my Talky Blogs and had with me at all times to document the moment for all my blog buddies to experience with me. Luckily, this is documented on video and is still posted on YouTube to this very day. Look it up. It's titled "TALKY BLOG: Koo Koo Woo Hoo." In fact, I just watched it right now and transcribed it word for word.

The following is my actual desperate call to action:

Blog buddies, I need your help! Ohhh, I'm heated. I am heated!

I just went to my beloved Koo-Koo-Roo....I love Koo-Koo-Roo. I'm koo-koo for it! It's because they have a squash, a butternut squash...

But they don't carry it anymore?!? What?!?

Now, I wouldn't dare give out the number [the 1-800 number flashes on the screen] for you to leave a voice mail for the fine people at Koo-Koo-Roo to say, "Please, bring back the squash."

I wouldn't dare ask my loyal, trusted blog buddies

to do that for me en masse...to bring back squash to Koo-Koo-Roo....

Then I drove home, halfheartedly ate my squashless dinner, and posted my Talky Blog to YouTube. When I awoke the next morning, it was a brave new world.

My blog buddies hadn't just united, overnight they had become a superpower of consumerism, a juggernaut of justice, a fierce force of feedback. By noon, my videotaped rant had thousands upon thousands of views on YouTube, and I had hundreds of comments from blog buddies who had called Koo-Koo-Roo to leave a message and join my very own Squash Squadron.

I nervously dialed Koo-Koo-Roo's customer service number again for myself. It was busy. I tried again. Again, it was busy. The third time I got through and couldn't believe what I heard on their prerecorded outgoing message. A woman's voice said, "Hello, and thank you for calling Koo-Koo-Roo. For store locations, press 1. For store hours, press 2. And to leave a message regarding Ross Mathews and our butternut squash, press 3."

Oh, holy crap, I thought to myself. *What have I done?*

My anxiety rose throughout the day as I read messages from blog buddies all over the world who had rallied on my behalf. People from Canada, Australia, Germany, and beyond—places millions of miles from a Koo-Koo-Roo—had reached past borders and across oceans to stand with me and make our voices heard.

I was freaking out now. I was certain this wasn't going to end well. It was hard not to think about the worst-case scenario. In a way, this had happened before when I tried to rally my troops of dedicated blog buddies to make me the spokesperson for Ross Dress For Less. I had assumed that the head honchos would be thrilled with the genius idea. I was wrong.

Rather than pat me on the back, the delightfully discounted department store slapped me with a cease-and-desist order from their lawyers. I still stand by that idea, by the way, and would totally forgive Ross Dress for Less if they changed their minds and reached out to me today. I mean, come on—I love fashion *and* a bargain! Plus, my name is Ross! Anyway, back to Koo-Koo-Roo...

Later that night, I got a message in my e-mail inbox from someone named Kathy with an e-mail address that ended in @kookooroo.com. She wrote that she worked for the company and wanted to speak with me as soon as possible.

Oh shit. I'd really done it now. Not only did I lose my scrumptious squash forever, but now I'd probably be outright banished for eternity from the kingdom of Koo-Koo-Roo. I'd gotten my feathers ruffled, taken a risk, and tried to fight against the status quo, all to have it explode in my face like squash cooked too long in the microwave.

Nervously, I dialed the number Kathy included in her e-mail. I was prepared for the worst, ready to have my dream of the perfect chicken restaurant cruelly plucked from me. Suddenly, she picked up. Again, this is dictated verbatim from the YouTube video (seriously, look it up).

KATHY : Ross, it is so good to finally talk to you in person...We're gonna bring it back!

ROSS : YAY!!!!!!!!!!!! WOO HOO!!!!!!!!!!!! So butter-nut squash is coming back to Koo-Koo-Roo?

KATHY : It is! But we want to thank you. We seriously want to name it the Butternut Ross Squash or something fun because it truly has become an inspiration. You're part of our Koo-Koo-Roo family.

ROSS : Wait. Are you kidding?!? Can you really call it Ross Squash?!?

KATHY : *(pausing, thinking)* Ross Squash?

ROSS : *(nodding feverishly)* Ross Squash!

Yep. That's really how it happened. And what followed was beyond my wildest fantasies. As the days went on, it all got even more exciting. Not only did Koo-Koo-Roo plan on bringing squash back with a new (and vastly improved) name, but they wanted to relaunch the veggie with a brand-new spokesperson: *me!*

I couldn't believe it! Some people wait a lifetime to become a spokesperson for a local chicken chain, but I was one of the lucky ones! Suddenly, my people were meeting with Koo-Koo-Roo's people about what kind of deal they could strike. I called my manager.

"Listen, don't charge them a dime. I don't want their money—this was never about a paycheck. Just make them promise to keep the Ross Squash on the menu forever and I'll do whatever they want."

"Are you sure, Ross?"

I was absolutely sure. "Yes, I'm absolutely sure."

It felt good to do the right thing.

After all, I was the leader of group of heroes. Koo-Koo-

Roo was playing chicken with us, but my flock of kind-hearted, squash-loving good Samaritans and I had clucked loudly enough to have created a better future for our children—a future filled with yummy, fiber-full, golden goodness. That was payment enough.

Within weeks, Ross Squash was on the menu and my face was posted on billboards and buses all over the greater Los Angeles area. I can't even tell you how weird it is, you guys, to look up while you're at a red light and come face-to-face with your own face.

If you think that's a weird experience, try waiting in line at your favorite restaurant and seeing your name on the menu (but it is kinda fun to order yourself). Now I know how Shirley Temple, that Reuben sandwich guy and Mrs. Patricia Melt must have felt.

What's even weirder than weird, though? About a month later at a charity function in Hollywood, Emmy-winning actor Eric McCormack (from *Will and Grace*) approached me from across the room, looked me dead in the eyes and proclaimed, "There he is, the man who brought back the squash! I was so furious when they took it away! I'm not even joking, Ross. Thank you!"

You're welcome, Emmy winner Eric McCormick. You're welcome.

God, victory is sweet—almost as sweet as the natural sugars in Ross Squash, now available at your local Koo-Koo-Roo.

Chapter Seventeen

COME OUT, COME OUT, WHEREVER YOU ARE

I realized I was gay in the shower one day with Barbra Streisand. It happened while I was lathering, rinsing, and repeating with Pert Plus (the original multitasker—shampoo and conditioner in one). As I was belting out the chorus to my favorite song from *Funny Girl*, "Oh my man, I love him so, he'll never know...," it hit me.

This was during my Barbra Streisand phase in high school. I'll always love her, but for a few months back then, her songs were on heavy rotation in my head.

On a clear day you can see forever, and on that particular day, just like Barbra Streisand's flawless voice, everything was crystal clear. It felt like an out-of-body experience as my perspective shifted and I saw myself for what I really was: a boy with impeccably cleaned and conditioned hair singing a stunning Streisand standard about the man who got away. I mean, duh. I can only compare it to staring at one of those Magic Eye posters. You know, those prints with the weird images that look like nothing more than static on an old TV until you manage to focus *just* right and suddenly an image of a dolphin seems to magically reveal itself when you least expect it. At that moment in the shower, I was like, "Oh, now I see..."

Suddenly everything made sense. My mind was racing. "*That's* why I always wanted Jason Priestley's home address! *That's* why I wish I was best friends with Delta Burke from *Designing Women*! *That's* why I'm not afraid to push the fashion envelope by boldly mixing plaids with stripes! And maybe, *just* maybe, *that's* why all my sexual fantasies are about men!"

DING DING DING! Either the microwave popcorn was ready, or I was on to something.

Now, despite being called "gay" and "fag" all my life by bullies and my boss in the spinach fields (remember chapter 1?), I didn't really comprehend what those words truly meant. To be honest, I'm not sure the kids saying them did, either. These days, if a kid is called gay, they have a friendly familiar face that comes to mind. They can think, *Oh, I'm like Ellen or Rosie or even that funny guy with the voice from* Chelsea Lately. *So* that's *what gay is.*

But, remember, this was a different time—there were no gay people on TV. Well, no *out* gay people at least. And there were certainly no gay role models in my small town, either. As naïve as it sounds, I kind of just didn't really know what being called gay meant. It was simultaneously mean and meaningless.

But back to my life-changing shower. As I let this epiphany wash over me, my life up to this point flashed before my eyes, like a movie montage after a mind-blowing, totally unexpected plot twist is revealed. Yes, all the puzzle pieces fit: The undeniable gravitational pull I felt toward not only female friends but just about anything considered dramatic or showbiz adjacent, the way certain parts of my young body tingled whenever I watched professional wrestling, and my penchant for adding a generous sprinkling of deliciously sweet golden raisins to my mother's homemade chicken salad sandwiches (trust me, try it and it'll rock your world).

Along with the suds that were swirling down the drain, also went any confusion as to why I had always felt slightly different from most everyone, with the possible exception of our town's premier hairstylist, the confirmed bachelor Mr. Franco.

I was at once a new person, and yet the same person I'd always been, if that makes any sense. It was instinctual, even my DNA was G-A-Y. *People, people who need people, are the luckiest people in the world...* And it just so happened that I needed people with penises. Big whoop.

The moment this shift occurred, I never looked back. I hopped on that gay train and went full steam ahead, right out of the closet! The first person I ever told was my ex-girlfriend, Carrie. She's the gorgeous gal whose girl groin I had agreed to gobble only a few months earlier. Remember her? The natural blonde who helped to crack open my closet door? Given our history, I felt that I could tell her anything without being judged. After all, she had "opened up" to me.

I revealed everything to her as we sat in my Ford Tempo in the parking lot of Cinema Five after seeing *Spice World: The Spice Girls Movie.* She had dressed up as Baby Spice. That was the one area where Carrie and I disagreed. I was a diehard Ginger Spice fan.

"Carrie, can I tell you something?" I took off my oversized sunglasses and put them in my Spice Girls unisex tote bag.

"Sure." She tilted her head sweetly. "You can tell me anything."

I took a deep breath. "I've never told anybody this before. Nobody. Not one person. Nobody at all."

"I know what *nobody* means, Ross. What is it?"

"Okay. The deal is, I think I'm pretty sure that I might possibly be, maybe, totally kind of sort of, well ... gay."

And then? Silence. Why didn't she gasp? Her face didn't even change at all. Frankly, this simply wasn't the dramatic reaction I was expecting.

Maybe she didn't hear me. "Um, hello? I just told you that I'm gay."

Finally she spoke. "Yeah, I heard you. Do you have any other breaking news? Like, I don't know, the sky is blue?"

And then we both burst into a fit of laughter, that wonderful kind of cathartic laughter that comes from a place deep within and makes you feel like a gigantic weight has been lifted off your chest.

Carrie knew I was gay. She'd known for a long time and never brought it up or forced me to talk about it, because she also knew that until I was ready to say it myself, I wouldn't be ready to hear it from anyone else.

What a feeling! My trusted confidante had increased my confidence and now I was free to be me! I can't tell you how amazing it felt the first time I saw a good-looking hunk in the mall while walking with Carrie and casually remarked, "Oh, he's cute!"

To anyone else, it might have seemed like a simple, offhand remark. But to me, it was a free expression of an aspect of myself that I'd never before articulated. It was bigger than big.

Cut to a few years later. I was a well-adjusted college student, out and proud on campus. With my freshman year behind me, I left Los Angeles and headed home to spend the summer at my parents' house. I felt guilty, like I was hiding something from them, probably because I was. Sure, all my friends knew I was gay, my professors knew I was gay, even the UPS guy knew I was gay, but my parents seemed clueless.

It was totally my fault that they didn't know. I was scared. I mean, you hear horror stories all the time about kids who are disowned and cast aside like a cashmere sweater with a little snag. Yes, as sad as it is, some parents consider their gay kids defective. Would mine think the same? Would they stop loving me? The bond between a parent and a child is supposed to be the epitome of unconditional love, but if that relationship hinges on not saying one single sentence, then there are, in fact, conditions. Would my parents' love for me be that fragile? The stakes were just too high.

I weighed my options. I wanted to live my life as an open book, but at what cost? By sharing my true self with the people who meant the most to me, I ran the risk of losing them altogether. But despite the possible worst-case scenario, I felt compelled to open up and let my family know the real me. You see, I had to, or else I wasn't being true to myself. This quote from Kurt Cobain sums it up perfectly: "I'd rather be hated for who I am, than loved for who I'm not."

I had faith in my parents. I knew they wouldn't hate me.

But I couldn't bear the thought of them loving me even a little less after I told them. I was the same exact person right before I said it, while I said it, and after it was said. But would they see me differently?

I remember lying on my mom's bed as she watched TV, my face buried into a pile of pillows. I kept thinking to myself, *You can do this. You can do this.*

Eventually my mom asked me, "Ross, are you all right?"

I'm not a highly emotional person, but before I even started speaking, my eyes were flooded with tears and I began to choke on my words. "Mom, promise you'll love me no matter what?"

"Oh, my God, sweetie, of course! What's going on?!?"

"Mom, I'm gay."

She looked confused. "Honey, I know. You already told me."

What the fuck was she talking about? "Mom, I never told you that!"

She was insistent. "Are you sure? I could have sworn you told me already."

"Mother, I would know whether I told you or not! It's kinda my story and I doubt I'd be freaking out and crying if I had already told you!"

She hugged me. "Oh God, honey. I've known since you were three years old! Shit, I don't care! I love you! We can go to downtown Mount Vernon right now and, swear to God, give me a sign that says, 'My Son Is Gay and I Love Him,' and I'll march up and down that street all night!"

If I was reading this in a book written about somebody else, I'd be rolling my eyes and murmuring, "Bullshit" under my breath right about now, but I swear on my dogs' lives (so you know I'm serious) that was *exactly* how it happened. I will love her always and always extra for that.

My football-loving, gun-toting dad took a little longer to come around. He was never much for discussing emotions at great length, so instead of a big dramatic scene, he eventually just sort of quietly accepted it. After he died, my mom told me she once overheard him talking to his best friend, another good old boy. She told me his friend asked him, "Is Ross gay?"

Without missing a beat, my dad matter-of-factly answered, "Yep."

That one-word answer spoke volumes. It's just one little word with only three letters, but knowing he said it is priceless to me because I knew it was his way of subtly expressing, *Yes, my son is gay and if you have something to say about it, we can take this outside and I'll kick your judgmental ass from here until next fuckin' Tuesday.*

I know that seems like a lot to read into a simple "Yep," but I knew my dad and I knew what he meant. So did my mom, and that was why she told me the story.

I know I'm one of the lucky ones. Thank goodness more and more parents are responding this way. But we can't deny the sad reality that for many, the reactions are very different.

One thing I've learned about life is that no one gets through it unscathed. You can't control much of anything. The only thing you can hope to control is how you react to situations. I'm often asked for advice on how parents and kids should handle these kinds of coming-out scenarios.

Personally, I can speak only for the kids. Be yourself and be respectful, but don't try to change for anyone. Because the truth is, there are some things we can't change about ourselves, even if we wanted to. And, really, why would you want to? You are not the problem. You are not defective. You are just right.

For parental advice, I defer to the best expert I know: my mom, Gaye. Yes, her name is Gaye. Gaye Mathews. Someone call the irony police. I called her while writing this and asked her the following question: "What advice would you offer the parent of a gay child?"

This was her answer. Please notice two things: (1) how adorably kindhearted she is, and (2) how her answer, even decades after the fact, is solely focused on the happiness and well-being of her son.

"Oh, wow. Well, I just wanted you to know that I was there and I wasn't surprised. Of course, my main concern was you. My only fear was that you could be hurt. I wanted to go out and fight for you, because I didn't know what else to do. It's just a protective instinct that parents have. I'd tell parents this: your job is to protect, support, and love your children no matter what, so just keep doing your job."

Moms—you've got to love 'em, right? And I've got a great one. Both my parents set an incredible example for me when it comes to acceptance and love. I'm blessed.

Before we hung up, I thanked her for her kind words of wisdom, reminding her how many people she might possibly help. But she wasn't finished and continued to elaborate enthusiastically (as she's known to do). "Having a gay son is fabulous! Everybody should have one. Ross, it's like you totally *get* me, you know? There's that special connection. Who else takes me to brunch and shopping and pedicures? And you always tell me the truth, even when I look like shit."

As my dad would've said, "Yep."

EPILOGUE

MAN UP!

I've been looking forward to retirement for as long as I can remember. Don't get me wrong, I'm not at all fed up with the workforce. On the contrary, I love what I get to do for a living. It's just that I can't wait to be an active senior citizen. Why? Because I think I'll be better at it than I have been at everything else in my entire life. If I'm anything, I'm a man built for grandkids, early-bird specials, and a personalized golf cart.

I have my retirement all planned out. I can't wait to sit on my lanai in a wicker chair (by the way, I always picture my retirement fantasies in the house from *The Golden Girls*) and reflect on my life. I'll have a wonderful, leathery tan and a long, silver ponytail even if I'm balding on top. Yes, I'll be *that* guy.

I'll also, for the record, insist on wearing only kimonos, turquoise jewelry, and slip-on orthopedic shoes at all times. I'll smell like rose oil mixed with Vicks VapoRub, and I'll live in my adopted hometown, the desert oasis known as Palm Springs. To make ends meet, I'll perform at a club I'll own called the Silver Fox Lounge, where I'll captivate the audience with old Hollywood stories from back in the day about when I hobnobbed with showbiz legends like Screech and Snooki. The adoring crowd of retirees will request that I sing old standards like the Spice Girls' classic "2 Become 1," and I'll close every show with my moving rendition of Christina Aguilera's "Beautiful." I don't promise to always remember the words to *every* song, but I guarantee it'll be as fabulous as it is elderly.

Most important, as I celebrate my golden years and wait to bask in the glory of that big lanai in the sky, I hope to reflect back and be proud of the life I've lived, from Balloon Day to this book and beyond. I want my kids and grandkids to know that every time I was scared of being mocked or put down or worried that I couldn't do something, I manned up and did it anyway.

This is how I define *man up*: you are what you are, and the sooner you stop hating what makes you unique and start celebrating it and using it to make you stand out from the crowd, the better your life will be. For some unknown reason, I was lucky enough to figure that out at an early age.

Not to be a total cheese ball, but I truly wish the same for you. And with any luck, maybe we'll run into each other in Palm Springs one day. You won't be able to miss me—I'll be the fabulously tan old man with a white wine spritzer, a lapdog, and a gigantic smile on my face...assuming, of course, I'm still physically capable of smiling after the facelift.

BONUS QUIZ!

Well, here we are at the end of the book! Can you believe it? Ahhhh. It feels good, doesn't it? I don't know about you, but I'm sore all over—my fingers from typing, my brain from thinking, and my face from smiling. Because, as enjoyable as this has been, writing a book is hard work!

I bet reading it all hasn't been a walk in the park, either (unless, of course, you're reading this while you're actually walking in a park). Thank you so, *so* much for joining me on this journey, dear reader. As a token of my appreciation, I'd like to leave you with a parting gift. No, not a gourmet gift basket filled with high-end tasty treats or a weekend getaway to a bed-and-breakfast in Boca Raton. You see, my gift to you is the gift of knowledge. Yep, that's right! It's time for the quiz I mentioned in the prologue. Please take out your No. 2 pencil and don't look at your neighbor's book.

What, you thought I was kidding? Oh no, I'm as serious about this as I am about Zac Efron's pecs, nonfat frozen yogurt, and correcting people when they misquote dialogue from *Pretty Woman*. Like, for reals. I don't joke about the important stuff.

I know a quiz might seem like overkill, but it is my deepest, most sincere hope that after you've digested the stories put forth in this book, a few precious kernels of wisdom shall remain intact. It's kinda like when you eat corn, you know what I mean?

I've designed these questions to help recap the more memorable moments of this book. Okay, who am I kidding? I just want to see if you really read the damn thing. I promise though, it'll be quick and painless. After all, we're just waxing nostalgic here, not waxing our hoo-hahs. Trust me, it'll be easy-breezy cover-to-cover, girl.

If you get a perfect score, I'll totally put you on my honor roll. No shame in being smart, people, and just about everybody looks sexy in glasses! Can you say "geek chic"?

Okay, here we go:

1. What are the names of my two paw-fect lil' pups?

   a. Mijo and Louise
   b. Lil' Loco and Wynndex
   c. Fart-Knocker and Mary Kate

2. Who is my Oscar-Winning BFF?

   a. That one guy who did sound for *Titanic*
   b. Gwyneth Paltrow
   c. Dwayne "The Rock" Johnson

3. Which employer fired me for "Grand Theft: Pajama Pants"?

a. Lane Bryant
b. Men's Warehouse
c. Arleen's Discount Jammy Emporium

4. What dish do I make every Thanksgiving?

a. Uncle Jerry's Creamed Corn
b. Cousin Tammy's Tuna Casserole
c. Nana's Potatoes

5. What was the name of my high school drug awareness troupe?

a. The Straight 'n' Narrows
b. Smack Attack!
c. Everything in Moderation Station

6. What book did I read while hunting with my dad?

a. The latest Jackie Collins romance
b. *Little House on the Prairie*
c. *Fifty Shades of Gay*

7. What caused me to make a complete ass of myself in front of Tiffani-Amber Thiessen?

a. A teeny mascara blob
b. An entire spinach salad in my teeth
c. Accidentally calling her "Screech"

8. Who was the first person I ever came out to?

a. Our family dog, Iggy
b. My ex-girlfriend, Carrie
c. I'm still in the closet

9. What would my name be if I were a Superhero?

    a. The Shrill
    b. Captain Fabulous
    c. The Inferior Decorator

10. What's the worst thing about a makeover?

    a. There is...
    b. ...nothing bad...
    c. ...about a makeover.
    d. ALL OF THE ABOVE

Answers: 1. a, 2. b, 3. a, 4. c, 5. a, 6. b, 7. a, 8. b, 9. a, 10. d

Okay, now it's time to find out what your score means!

0 correct answers: Huh?!?

You are dead to me.

1–3 correct answers: Rereading Is Fundamental.

I have to say, I'm very disappointed in you. It's like I slaved over a hot stove all day, whipping up a gourmet dinner, and you took one measly bite. Remember when Tyra Banks freaked out on *America's Next Top Model* that one time and screamed, *"I was rooting for you! We were all rooting for you"*?

Well, I always thought she was overreacting...until now. The great news? Just like *America's Next Top Model All Stars*, there's still a chance for you. Go back to page 1 and reread this very important book. Only, this time, please take notes.

4–7 correct answers: A for Average.

Okay, not bad. You're kind of like sex with me—not the best, not the worst, but at least you tried and chances are you laughed a little.

8–10 correct answers: Bravo, Bookworm!

OMG! You like me! You really like me! All my hard work paid off! I know it's very difficult to concentrate and read a book, especially these days with the TV and Twitter and whatnot. I'm very impressed, dear reader! By the way, I've spoken to my lawyer, so you should probably keep an eye out for my restraining order. Your obsession with me is starting to freak me out. I mean, stalker much?

AFTERWORD

By Chelsea Handler

Whether or not I'm partial to gay men is a non-starter. The bottom line is that Ross Mathews is my favorite gay *person*. Is he defined by his homosexuality? Absolutely. But if I had to name the second thing I love most about Ross, it would be his unbridled enthusiasm.

I met him eight years ago at the *Tonight Show*, and after seeing his correspondence work on Jay Leno, I demanded that he do stand-up comedy. He was resistant to the idea but I forced his hand, body, and mind to at least give it a twirl. We spent a week in Arizona with him as my opening act, and even though he didn't love stand-up, I watched him sashay up and down the dirty aisles of that comedy club like a toddler wearing a tiara.

He brought along his best friend Kimmy with whom we shared our days and pre-show sushi dinners. This was before I knew sushi wasn't something you ordered on a daily basis while sequestered in a landlocked state. This was when Ross revealed to me that he had never given or received penetration; a straight-up virgin.

I had never met a virgin before and was extremely concerned. He reassured me that he had had a myriad of "almost" sex situations with women, which really knocked me for a loop-de-loop. "What person with female parts would think you're straight?"

He regaled me with the first time he went downtown on a girl, or rather tried, and then almost vomited on her. I was horrified. What a victory lap for that poor girl.

I knew if he was ever going to have the guts to show a man his body, I would have to stay in his life and help him gain the confidence one requires to sleep around.

I am as proud to call Ross one of my dear friends many years later as I am proud to be able to publish his very first book. I can unabashedly admit that I have seen Ross turn from a young talented boy into the gay man's Popeye.

Acknowledgments

A lady by the name of Chelsea Handler is responsible for this book's existence. Honey bunny, I love you. You have given me so much, from the opportunity to really develop my point of view to a platform from which to express it and so much more. Everyone knows how funny you are, but I am honored to know firsthand how generous, kind, and loving you are. I also loved that you would call me at seven in the morning from your treadmill with notes on this book. I just love a lady who's hands-on.

Jay Leno is responsible for anybody knowing who I am in the first place. Jay, if you hadn't taken a risk on a wacky intern over a decade ago, I have no idea where I would be right now. Who would have thought that over eleven years after we met, I'd be writing about you in a book about my life? Unreal. I am eternally grateful.

These two amazing people, Jay and Chelsea, have been instrumental in the course of my life and career. A mere thank-you seems like much too simple a phrase to express the gratitude I feel, but thank you both so, *so* much.

Also, the people with whom I work on both Jay's and Chelsea's shows continue to inspire and support me. Thank you to Debbie Vickers, Tom Brunelle, Anthony Caleca, Joe Medeiros, Jack Cohen, Scott Atwell, Steve Ridgeway, Larry Jacobson, Kevin Frasier, Ken Gomez, Izzy Centeno, Sue Murphy, Michael Cox, Brad Wollack, Rene Mooshy, and all the hilarious and talented people I've had the privilege of performing with on both *The Tonight Show* and *Chelsea Lately*. Rising up to your level is an honor.

I still can't believe I even know Gwyneth Paltrow, let alone know her well enough to have her e-mail address. And I find it unfathomable that I would have the audacity to e-mail Gwyneth Paltrow and ask her to write the foreword in my book. A book that, by the way, contains an entire chapter about how creepily obsessed I am with her. And it is laughable that she agreed to do it, even after reading it. But that's why I love her. She's been a true BFF to me since the day we met. I love you, lady.

Thank you to the people who have inspired me as I've watched hours upon hours upon gazillions of hours of TV throughout my life, including: Jay, Howard Stern, Regis Philbin, Kathie Lee Gifford, Rosie O'Donnell, Rikki Lake, Steve Edwards, Jillian Barberie, and Dorothy Lucey (formerly) from *Good Day LA*, and Oprah...Oprah...Oprah...

A special thank-you goes out to Michael Broussard, my literary agent, and Beth de Guzman, my editor, as well as everyone else at Grand Central Publishing. Thanks for being in my corner and for guiding me so well.

Thank you to all my agents at CAA for their constant support and guidance. You're all the best in the business.

Thank you to everyone at E! for always being so supportive and kind.

Austin Young shot the cover photograph for this book. From the first time I saw his amazing work, I knew I wanted him to shoot my first book cover. Ten years later, he did so, and he did an awesome job.

My manager, Mark Degenkolb, has been a constant in my life for years. Thank you for being the person at the front lines of our business who not only has the job of giving me the good news, but knows how to deliver the bad news as well. Thank you, also, for that time you told me I was getting fat again.

My mom is a kind, giving caretaker and a real trouper. Thank you for not only loving me no matter what, but also never once asking me to remove something from this book. I love you!

Thank you to my brother, Eric, for allowing me to share our stories and for being a major source of support. I love you, buddy.

I wish my father could've read this book. He would've thought it was hilarious. I miss you, Dad, and I love you.

There are so many others to thank for their kindness, friendship, love, and support throughout my life, including: Kim, Boni, Kai, Ryan MacD, Kathy Clark Smith, Mr. Zickler, Ms. Smith, Ms. Watson, Mac, Karen Paterka, Dr. and Sistah Neighbor, Dan Pasternack, Mike Laponis, Dr. Kim Martin, Esther, Nikki Boyer, Daria Benedict, Susan and Butch Kisler, Bill and Mike, Arleen and Pat, Diana Degenkolb, Don, Jackie Collins, Carlos, Christina, Uncles Jon, Billy, and Jimmy, Aunts Jill, Sandy, Betty, Marilyn, and

Rosie, Grandma Bonnie, Bunka, both my grandfathers, my cousins, all the blog buddies, and so many others. I am so lucky to know you all.

Jackie Beat and Taya Faber, two of the funniest people to grace this planet, consulted with me during my writing process. Together, laughing in my house as I typed, we became a troupe of misfit writers determined to tell a funny, honest, and worthwhile story. Look at what we did, you guys! I'm proud of us and I love you both.

My paw-fect pups, Louise and Mijo, are always there for me with a million kisses. Daddy loves you!

To my Salvador, who thinks I'm absolutely ridiculous. On our first date, as I became frazzled while looking for parking, he told me, "You need to calm down." He's been that kind of consistently calming presence ever since. Thank you, Salvador, for building a life with me and for being patient as I finished this book. You are an essential source of strength for me. I love you so much.

And finally, to my future children, I will always love you, no matter what. Here's hoping, even after you read this book one day in the distant future, you'll extend me the same courtesy. I can't wait to meet you.

If I forgot anyone, I'm sorry. It's like that time Hilary Swank won the Oscar for *Boys Don't Cry* and totally forgot to thank her husband, what's-his-name. They ended up getting divorced. So, if I did forget you, let's be honest—it doesn't look good for us. Thanks anyway, though.

Mathews out.

More from A Chelsea Handler/ Borderline Amazing Publishing

Available in March 2014

More from A Chelsea Handler/ Borderline Amazing Publishing

Available now

More from A Chelsea Handler/
Borderline Amazing Publishing

Available now

What's so funny?

Pick up a copy today.

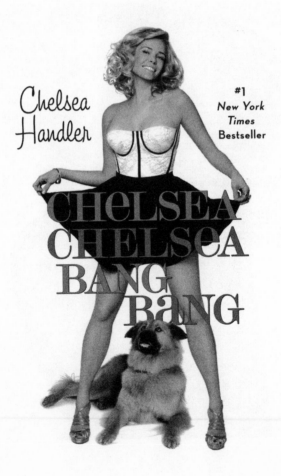